Sue Morris is a CBT-trained clinical psychologist and director of bereavement services at Dana-Farber Cancer Institute, Boston, USA. She has previously worked in community health and private practice in Sydney, Australia. She is the author of *An Introduction to Coping with Grief* and has co-authored four self-help books about relationships and motherhood.

The aim of the **Overcoming** series is to enable people with a range of common problems and disorders to take control of their own recovery programme.

Each title, with its specially tailored programme, is devised by a practising clinician using the latest techniques of cognitive behavioural therapy – techniques that have been shown to be highly effective in changing the way patients think about themselves and their problems.

Many books in the Overcoming series are recommended by the UK Department of Health under the Books on Prescription scheme.

Other titles in the series include:

OVERCOMING ALCOHOL MISUSE, 2ND EDITION
OVERCOMING ANGER AND IRRITABILITY, 2ND EDITION
OVERCOMING ANOREXIA NERVOSA
OVERCOMING ANXIETY, 2ND EDITION
OVERCOMING BODY IMAGE PROBLEMS INCLUDING BODY DYSMORPHIC DISORDER
OVERCOMING BULIMIA NERVOSA AND BINGE-EATING, 3RD EDITION
OVERCOMING CHILDHOOD TRAUMA
OVERCOMING CHRONIC FATIGUE
OVERCOMING CHRONIC PAIN
OVERCOMING DEPERSONALIZATION AND FEELINGS OF UNREALITY
OVERCOMING DEPRESSION, 3RD EDITION
OVERCOMING DISTRESSING VOICES
OVERCOMING GAMBLING ADDICTION, 2ND EDITION
OVERCOMING HEALTH ANXIETY
OVERCOMING HOARDING
OVERCOMING INSOMNIA AND SLEEP PROBLEMS
OVERCOMING LOW SELF-ESTEEM, 2ND EDITION
OVERCOMING MILD TRAUMATIC BRAIN INJURY AND POST-CONCUSSION SYMPTOMS
OVERCOMING MOOD SWINGS
OVERCOMING OBSESSIVE COMPULSIVE DISORDER
OVERCOMING PANIC, 2ND EDITION
OVERCOMING PARANOID AND SUSPICIOUS THOUGHTS, 2ND EDITION
OVERCOMING PERFECTIONISM, 2ND EDITION
OVERCOMING RELATIONSHIP PROBLEMS, 2ND EDITION
OVERCOMING SEXUAL PROBLEMS, 2ND EDITION
OVERCOMING SOCIAL ANXIETY AND SHYNESS, 2ND EDITION
OVERCOMING STRESS
OVERCOMING TRAUMATIC STRESS, 2ND EDITION
OVERCOMING WEIGHT PROBLEMS
OVERCOMING WORRY AND GENERALISED ANXIETY DISORDER, 2ND EDITION
OVERCOMING YOUR CHILD'S FEARS AND WORRIES
OVERCOMING YOUR CHILD'S SHYNESS AND SOCIAL ANXIETY
STOP SMOKING NOW, 2ND EDITION

OVERCOMING GRIEF

2nd Edition

*A self-help guide using
cognitive behavioural techniques*

OVERCOMING

SUE MORRIS

ROBINSON

ROBINSON

First published in Great Britain in 2018 by Robinson

A CIP catalogue record for this book
is available from the British Library.

IMPORTANT NOTE
This book is not intended as a substitute for medical advice or treatment.
Any person with a condition requiring medical attention should consult a
qualified medical practitioner or suitable therapist.

ISBN: 978-1-47214-043-2

Typeset in Bembo by Initial Typesetting Services, Edinburgh
Printed and bound in Great Britain by Clays Ltd, Elcograf S.p.A.

Papers used by Robinson are from well-managed forests and
other responsible sources

Robinson
An imprint of
Little, Brown Book Group
Carmelite House
50 Victoria Embankment
London EC4Y 0DZ

An Hachette UK Company
www.hachette.co.uk
www.littlebrown.co.uk

Contents

Acknowledgments   vii

A note of caution   ix

1   Your story   1

2   Grief's hold   12

3   Permission to grieve   39

4   Regaining control   63

5   Choose to act   101

6   Difficult conversations   138

7   Maintaining a connection   175

8   The 'firsts'   207

9   Your new path   245

10   For those who care   275

Appendix 1: Keeping a journal   309

Appendix 2: Useful frameworks   313

Appendix 3: Resources   320

References   330

Further reading   333

Index   337

Acknowledgements

Over the past twenty years, I have had the privilege to work with many bereaved individuals at a time when they were most vulnerable and alone. I would like to thank them for telling me their stories about how the deaths of their loved ones impacted their lives. I would also like to thank my many friends and relatives in the USA, UK and Australia who also shared their stories about grief and loss. In particular, I would like to thank my colleagues – past and present – at Old Colony Hospice and Dana-Farber Cancer Institute in Boston, USA, where I learnt so much and continue to do so about death and dying and the need to raise awareness about the importance of bereavement care. I am also very grateful to my friend and Australian colleague Jo Lamble, who read the original manuscript. Also, I would like to thank the staff at Robinson, for their guidance and support and the invitation to write this second edition. Finally, a big thank you to my family and friends for their continued encouragement – especially David and our daughters, and to my mother and father who taught me first-hand about life and death.

Sue Morris

A note of caution

Self-help books can never replace professional help if that is what is needed. But they can provide you with a better understanding of the problems you are facing, and offer suggestions about making changes.

Grief is a difficult topic, so reading a self-help book about the subject can be challenging. It is unlikely that anyone who is grieving is going to 'enjoy' reading a book about grief. Irrespective of when your loved one died, *Overcoming Grief* may stir up a lot of strong emotions. While feelings of deep sadness are a normal and expected reaction to the death of a loved one, it is important that you don't force yourself to deal with issues about their death before you are ready.

A self-help book about grief might not provide enough support for some people. If at any time you feel hopeless about your situation, or think that you are getting worse, then seek professional help immediately.

Be aware of the following warning signs that you might need professional help.

* Feeling as though you have been 'stuck' for some time

- Feeling increasingly depressed
- Feeling hopeless about your future
- Thinking about suicide or not being here anymore
- Thinking that life isn't worth living
- Making plans about how you could commit suicide
- Withdrawing from friends and family
- Experiencing marked disturbances in your sleep or appetite
- Feeling panicky, anxious or agitated
- Ruminating over the same thoughts or worries
- Having great difficulty carrying out your day-to-day activities
- Avoiding people or places that remind you of your loved one
- Having difficulty going to work, university or school
- Relying heavily on alcohol or other substances

Seek help from a doctor, grief counsellor or clinical psychologist if you experience any of these symptoms consistently, for more than a week or two, and if you feel as though you are getting worse. Coming to terms with the death of a loved one is hard work both emotionally and physically, and there is nothing shameful about seeking help.

1

Your story

My grief has consumed me. My husband died suddenly, five months ago, and I can't begin to describe the emptiness I feel. Each morning I wake up hoping to find it was just a bad dream. It's a struggle to get through the day and I'm not sure what to do. When I heard that my local hospice was running a bereavement group, I mustered what little energy I had and went. I needed to do something, anything.

LEE, 63

At the support group nine men and women were seated at the table. Each had come with their own story to tell – stories full of pain, heartache and intense sadness. They were uncertain and their emotions were raw. At first the room was quiet, but before long these strangers were sharing their stories about the death of their loved one. Peter was there because his wife of thirty-five years had died six weeks earlier from lung cancer; Kate's 38-year-old son had died four months ago in a car accident; and Beth had come because the first anniversary of her mother's death was approaching and she felt as though she was getting worse. Even though each of their stories was different and their grief unique, they had come because they needed to do something to help ease their pain. They had come because they felt alone and wanted to connect with people who were experiencing something similar. Lee had come because she didn't know what else to do.

Who has died in your life that has led you to this book? Maybe it was your partner or spouse, your son or daughter, your father or mother, or a special friend or relative. No matter who died or how they died, your story and your grief are unique. The pain you are experiencing cannot be compared or minimised. It doesn't matter how old the person was who died or that someone else's situation seems worse than yours. If you loved them or they were a significant part of your life, then your pain is real and your grief valid.

In psychological terms, *grief* is defined as 'the anguish experienced after significant loss, usually the death of a beloved person'. Finding ways to express your anguish or pain and reconcile your loved one's death are important parts of grieving. You might need to tell your story over and over again, or search for answers in an attempt to understand what happened. And you may have to wrestle with difficult memories, regrets and 'if onlys'. Even though no one can grieve for you, *Overcoming Grief* can help you work out what it is that you need to do to get through this difficult time in your life.

Grief is defined as the anguish experienced after significant loss, usually the death of a beloved person.

What is *your* story?

Each person has a different story to tell about how their loved one died and the impact it had on their life. Death can be expected, or it can be sudden and tragic. Regardless of how your loved one died, being able to tell your story – either publicly or privately – will help you make sense of what has happened, and hopefully allow you to accept how your life has changed.

There are several important and different components to consider when you think about your story. Those listed below will be addressed throughout *Overcoming Grief*.

- Who died?
- How did they die?
- Was their death expected or unexpected?
- What have you lost with the death of this person?
- Who can support you as you grieve?
- What would your loved one want for you now?
- Which direction do you see your life taking now?

Even if you don't consider yourself to be a 'talker', it's still important to ask yourself whether or not you have had the opportunity to talk about the death of your loved one.

Some people don't feel the need to talk at all and prefer to think through things on their own, whereas others need to talk to express their thoughts and feelings. If you are someone who wants to talk about what happened, often the hardest part is finding someone who can truly listen to you rather than telling you what to do.

It's common for people to say that in the beginning they were able to talk about the death, but that as time went on they found it increasingly difficult, for fear of burdening those around them. As a whole, Western society isn't very good at supporting those who are grieving. This probably has a lot to do with the fact that many people tend to find the subject of death uncomfortable, especially because there is nothing that can be done to 'fix' the problem. There is also a general perception that grief is something you can get over easily and in a relatively short period of time, in much the same way as you'd recover from an infection. Unfortunately this misperception is perpetuated because people, despite their best intentions, don't really understand the complexity of grief. What often ends up happening is that they become impatient with the bereaved person's so-called 'lack of progress' and say things that imply they should be better by now. The problem is that grief is not widely understood – grieving is a process of adjustment and new learning that cannot be hurried.

*Grieving is a process of adjustment and new
learning that cannot be hurried.*

Four recurring themes

When someone is grieving, especially if it is their first experience of the death of someone close to them, not knowing what to expect or how best to handle certain situations often intensifies their grief. Many people report that feeling they have little control over what is happening to them or around them is a significant factor that contributes to their anguish.

Throughout the book there are four major themes that provide a framework to help you understand grief more fully. These themes – covered separately over the following pages – will help you work out where to focus your attention so that you can begin to regain some control in your life.

1. Your grief is unique
2. Grieving gives you the time and space to learn to live without your loved one
3. You *can* overcome grief's hold
4. It's up to you.

1. Your grief is unique

No two people will experience the death of a loved one in the same way, so it's impossible to truly know another person's pain or sense of loss. And it's difficult to predict how you will grieve because it depends on many factors. These include your personality, the way you tend to deal with problems, the way you think about things that happen in your life, the nature of the relationship you had with the person who died, and the circumstances surrounding their death. Even if you have experienced the death of other people in your life, your grief will be different each time. What makes grief so complex is that with the death of one person, those left behind experience many different kinds of loss. If you accept that your grief is unique, then it makes sense that there is no one way to grieve. Part of the struggle of grieving involves working out what *you* need to do to adjust to life without that special person.

2. Grieving gives you the time and space to learn to live without your loved one

From the very moment you learn about the death of your loved one, your life changes forever. The amount of change relates to the degree of adjustment and new learning that you have to undertake. Too often others expect you to 'get back to normal' within weeks. This is unrealistic because your life has changed and it will never be the same as it was before. The path you were once walking together is no longer an option. It is as if you have been forced on to a new path, not of your choosing. The process of grieving is healthy and adaptive. It gives you the time and space to adjust to the many changes that result from the death of your loved one, both at a physical and an emotional level. Even though you may never 'get over' the death of your loved one, it is possible to learn to live without them physically in your life and to find meaning again.

3. You can overcome grief's hold

During the first few months you might feel as if your grief has a life of its own, with total control over you. You may feel that there is absolutely nothing you can do to loosen its grip. Often people say that they feel helpless and powerless, and describe a feeling of being 'out of control' which can be very disconcerting. Trying to regain a sense of control and order in your life will help you as you grieve. The aim is to shift the balance of power so that, gradually, you can begin to overcome the hold grief has on you. There are many strategies that can help you start to take control of your life again, which tackle your thoughts about the death as well as your behaviour.

4. It's up to you

One of the hardest things about grieving is that no one else can do it for you, which can feel very lonely and isolating. At times you may wonder whether what you are experiencing is 'normal'. You might have lots of unanswered questions and you may have many well-meaning friends who tell you that they *know* how you are feeling and what you *should* be doing. But because grieving is something you need to do for yourself, the best advice is to take things slowly and pay attention to your inner voice. Listen to your grief. Even though, logically, you know your loved one has died, you need time to reconcile what has happened and to work out what is best for you. Unfortunately, at a time when you are likely to be most vulnerable, grieving requires you to become your best advocate by speaking up for what you need.

Is it really possible to overcome grief?

Although the title of this book is *Overcoming Grief*, you might be wondering whether it is possible ever to overcome your grief. The title is meant to suggest that you can do things to help yourself overcome the intense, raw pain that is your grief, so you can continue to live your life in a meaningful way. It is not meant to imply that you will get over the death of your loved one. Grieving is an ongoing process that knows no time limits. Hopefully, one day, you will get to a point where you will be able to say to yourself that you feel as though you have overcome your grief – or the hold it had on you – while knowing that your loved one and the life you shared will never be forgotten.

It is possible to do things that can help you overcome the intense, raw pain that is your grief.

I was three years old when my mother died. I was so young that I was not able to appreciate the profound effect her death would have on my life. My youngest sister was also to die. She was seven years old when she died from osteomyelitis of the spine. We had been separated since my mother's death and at the age of ten I tried to understand death. The sadness of the funeral service and seeing the little blue coffin affected me greatly and I became withdrawn and constantly wondered if I could also die.

After I finished school I completed my General Nursing training. Having to deal with death on a daily basis gave me the strength later to face my husband's illness and subsequent death. Only with the expertise of devoted doctors, and the love and support of our family and friends, was he able to rally through difficult times. As a family we endured the relentless phases of his demise until one day, with his children and me by his side, he died slowly and with dignity. Again, I was to feel this great loss of a person who meant so much to me. For so long my daily nursing duties had consumed my waking hours caring for my husband, and now nothing seemed to matter. I lost interest in everything but felt I had to be strong for my children and grandchildren.

The frightening dreams I had before his death, of a large black form standing over my bed, never occurred again. In time I resumed a better sleeping pattern. The support of my family and friends helped me find comfort in knowing that I had been a special part of a well-lived life. Gradually, my constant visions of my husband in his last days are fading and being replaced by memories of the strong, healthy, loving person he was when I first met him some fifty-four years ago.

THELMA, 74

How to use this book

Step by step, *Overcoming Grief* will show you how to begin to take charge of your life again, using a 'tool box' approach. Unfortunately there is no magic cure. And even though you know there's nothing that can be done to bring back your loved one, you can begin to take action to overcome the hold grief has on you. As you read on, you'll find a number of different exercises or 'tools' in each chapter that will help you grieve the loss of your loved one. These exercises are based on the psychological treatment model known as cognitive behavioural therapy (CBT). They focus on your thoughts and behaviour, not only about the death of your loved one, but also about building a new life for yourself. It's a good idea to use a journal to write down your answers to these exercises. This way you can keep a record of your work and track your progress. And because each chapter builds on the one before, it's best to read through the book from beginning to end, rather than dipping in and out.

SUGGESTION: USE A JOURNAL

There are a number of written exercises in *Overcoming Grief*, and as you work through them it can be valuable to record your answers in a journal or book that you can look back over in months to come. This way you keep your answers together, which can help you track your progress. You may

---

like to buy a book that has meaning to you – maybe one that is a special colour or which has a picture on the cover that reminds you of your loved one. Another idea is to use a loose-leaf folder and make your own cover using photos of your loved one or other keepsakes.

Summary

- Tell your story
- Your grief is unique
- Grieving gives you the time and space to learn to live without your loved one
- Grief has a life of its own
- You *can* overcome grief's hold
- It's up to you

2

Grief's hold

It's important to understand the nature of grief because it is far more complex than most people think. In fact grief seems as though it has a life of its own. When someone you love dies, the intense emotional and physical pain you feel is often unbearable and indescribable – like nothing you've known before. You may think you're going crazy. Or you might not feel anything – you may just be completely numb. It's likely that you will experience many different emotions all at once. Unfortunately when someone dies, there is nothing anyone can do to change what has happened. Coming to terms with the finality of death is very hard work both emotionally and physically – there is no way around grief. But you can help yourself through this difficult time by working out what you need to do to lessen the hold grief has over you. This may sound like an impossible task but the next few chapters will show you how to begin.

The early days

In the early days after someone close to you dies, grief's hold can be powerful and all-encompassing. Many people describe their emotions as paralysing. Not only is grief characterised by deep sadness, but also by an intense longing or yearning to be with that person again. During this period it can feel like there is nothing you can do to lessen grief's hold.

If someone you loved has died recently, you are likely to experience a number of intense physical and emotional reactions – possibly all at once or in quick succession. Table 2.1 lists some of the most common responses.

TABLE 2.1 PHYSICAL AND EMOTIONAL REACTIONS TO THE DEATH OF A LOVED ONE

Physical reactions	Emotional reactions
Numbness	Intense sadness
Headaches	Disbelief
Nausea	Despair
A racing heart	Shock
Muscle tension	Worry
Aches and pains	Anguish
Difficulty sleeping	Anger
Difficulty eating/loss of appetite	Guilt

Physical reactions	Emotional reactions
Agitation	Regret
Restlessness	Peace
Fear	Emptiness
Panic	Pining or yearning
Crying, sobbing	Confusion
Gastrointestinal disturbance (diarrhoea/cramps)	Relief

These lists are by no means exhaustive. And you might find that you experience only some of these reactions, or some more than others. Whatever you experience is perfectly normal – remember that your grief is unique. If the death of your loved one was unexpected, shock and disbelief might be the main reactions you feel at first as your brain tries to make sense of what has happened. If their death was expected, especially after a long illness, you may feel a sense of relief and peace knowing that your loved one is no longer suffering. Often people question whether they are wrong to feel this way. The answer is definitely not. It is not uncommon to experience intense sadness and relief both at the same time. Some people say that they feel guilty about feeling relieved, but relief is as valid an emotion as any other. Being able to articulate your thoughts and feelings is an important part of grieving, as you will see in Chapter 3.

How long will I feel like this?

Almost everybody who is grieving asks, *How long will I feel like this?* Most of us, in anything we do, like to know where something begins and where it ends. We like to be in control and have order in our lives. Unfortunately, when you are grieving it is impossible to know how long your pain will last. Most people report that their grief comes in waves and that the intensity and frequency of these waves lessen over time. One of the defining features of these waves of grief is a pining or yearning for their loved one, which can be emotionally and physically painful.

Holding on to the knowledge that eventually your pain will ease is important as you face your grief. Even though there are no set timelines to follow, many people who are grieving report that in the beginning they functioned as though they were on automatic pilot, and felt as though they had little or no control over what was happening to them. Gradually, as they learnt to live without the person who died they found that their pain lessened and they were able to find enjoyment in their life again. How long it takes will be different for everyone.

It is important to hold on to the knowledge that eventually your pain will ease.

AUTOMATIC PILOT

In the days following the death of a loved one, people often describe themselves as being on 'automatic pilot' where they are just 'going through the motions'. They might not be able to remember who came to the funeral or what they did on a particular day. They might feel as though they cannot switch off their thoughts or feelings and may have great difficulty sleeping. These bodily changes and the sense of being on 'automatic pilot' can in part be explained by the activation of the 'fight or flight' response. When somebody learns of the death of a loved one, their body interprets the news as a major stressful event or threat, and responds by releasing the hormone adrenaline to help them deal with the threat. Adrenaline increases your heart and breathing rates and primes your muscles, preparing you for a fight, or to run away (flight). The body also releases other chemicals, which temporarily help to numb the pain. It is not uncommon for people to say that they feel worse somewhere between four and six weeks after the death. It's believed that what is actually happening is that these chemicals are returning to their normal levels and the pain of the grief is being felt to its full extent. At this point the reality of the death is also setting in, especially as friends and family begin to call or visit less often. As other people's lives return to normal, the bereaved person is likely to notice the absence of their loved one even more. And it may feel as though grief has an even stronger hold.

Soon after she died I did everything. I made the funeral arrangements, organised her affairs and visited the lawyer to make a new will. Now, six weeks on, I feel worse than ever. I didn't feel anything in the beginning; I just did

what I needed to do. Now I feel everything. I am angry
– angry with God for taking her from me and angry with
the doctors because they could not save her. I can't stop
crying and wonder how I will go on without her.

ALAN, 69

CONTROL

The notion of control plays a central role in grief. In most cases, when someone dies you have little control over the events that lead to their death and the intense pain that follows. Feeling out of control is never nice as it makes you feel vulnerable. That is why it's important to work out what you need to do to regain some control at a time when you feel as though you have very little control.

It is useful to think of a funnel in relation to controlling your grief. As each week passes, hopefully you can do things that help you feel a little more in control of your pain, and which allow you to funnel or channel your grief so that it becomes more bearable. The strategies outlined in the following chapters are designed to help increase your sense of control. These include methods that focus on the way you are thinking about the death and your future, as well as others that target your behaviour.

When my little boy died I remember just wanting some-
one to give me a sleeping pill that would let me sleep
until I could bear to think about what happened. Now,
many years later, the feeling I can still vividly remember

is that of just wanting to throw a huge tantrum – as a child would do after their favourite toy had been taken from them. It felt so primitive but I suppose it was just the realisation that I had absolutely no power or control over what had happened.

KATHI, 48

MEDICATION

When the reality of a loved one's death begins to set in, many people wonder whether they will ever again enjoy their life in some way. In those first few months it is not uncommon to experience sleeping difficulties, or to feel depressed or anxious. Even though these are all usual reactions to the death of someone close, some people wonder whether medication may help them feel better or recover more quickly. There are many differing opinions about whether people who are grieving should take medication given that grief is not an illness, especially antidepressant medication. As a general guideline, people should be assessed individually by their doctor. If you have a history of clinical depression, anxiety disorders or a serious medical condition, you should let your doctor know of your loved one's death, especially if it was unexpected. They might want to monitor your mood or health more closely than usual and adjust any medication accordingly.

SUGGESTION: LET YOUR DOCTOR KNOW

If you have a regular doctor, make an appointment to see them. Ask someone to contact them on your behalf to inform them of the death of your loved one. They might want to make some recommendations about your care during this difficult time.

If you are having trouble sleeping you might want to ask your doctor about short-term sleeping medication. Experiencing ongoing sleep disturbance is likely to compound your grief, especially as it much harder to shut off racing thoughts when you are trying to get to sleep. But it's important to avoid becoming dependent on such medication. For more on sleep disturbances see Chapter 5. The same also applies to anxiety. If you're feeling very anxious or panicky, talk to your doctor about the possibility of medication to manage these feelings. But remember that these medications should be used with caution, and that none of them can take away the pain of losing your loved one.

When you are grieving it is perfectly normal to feel depressed, but these feelings are very different from being diagnosed with clinical depression. This is a serious, debilitating disorder. Feeling very sad, down, blue, apathetic and unmotivated are all expected and usual reactions to loss. But there are a number of reasons why your doctor might want to consider prescribing medication or referring you to a psychiatrist or clinical psychologist for therapy:

- A history of clinical depression
- Thoughts or expressions of suicide
- A prolonged grief reaction that doesn't appear to be easing
- Dealing with a sudden and unexpected death
- Dealing with a violent death
- An ongoing inability to function and to carry out daily tasks
- Feelings of hopelessness about the future

Grief is not the same as clinical depression even though you may feel 'depressed'.

Understanding grief

How we think about life affects how we think about death, and also how we grieve. With today's medical advances most people expect that children will outlive their parents, that most of us will live long and healthy lives, and hopefully that we will die peacefully in our sleep. When someone dies suddenly and without warning, as in sudden infant death, accidents, suicide, homicide and from undiagnosed medical conditions, many of these basic assumptions about life are challenged. In the same way, the diagnosis of a terminal illness and the subsequent death can also challenge a person's belief about the world, as in Mary's case.

My husband always had his annual medical check-up and really took care of himself. He seemed so healthy. I just don't understand why the doctors didn't diagnose his condition earlier. It's so unfair. I'll never get over it.

MARY, 56

When your assumptions are challenged by illness and death, a discrepancy occurs between what you hoped or expected to happen in your life and what actually happened. How readily you are able to reconcile the death and make some kind of sense of it will impact on your grieving. The greater the discrepancy, the more difficult it can be to come to terms with the death of a loved one. This is one reason why the death of a young child is considered to be one of the greatest losses – it challenges all our beliefs about life and death and the way we think things 'should' be.

When someone dies suddenly and without warning, many of the basic assumptions we hold about life are challenged.

The wave-like pattern of grief

Even though no one can take away your pain at this time, understanding some of what you are experiencing can help ward off the feeling that you are going crazy, and increase your sense of control. Whether the death of your loved one was expected or sudden, many people find it helpful to think of grief as following a wave-like pattern.

Imagine that your grief is like a series of waves, joined together to form one continuous wave-like pattern. This pattern represents the ups and downs of grief that you'll have to endure over time. The strength or height of the waves at any point varies between people. It's common for many people to report in the weeks following their loved one's death that the waves are very intense and that there isn't much of a break between them. As time goes on, the waves decrease in intensity and hit a little less often. Gradually the break between each wave starts to get longer, and you may even think things are getting 'a little better'. Then, out of the blue, a big wave can strike again and it will seem as if things are getting worse. It's typical for something to trigger these large waves or 'trigger waves'. This can be anything from a significant date or event to hearing a favourite song on the radio. Changes in the season, seeing a stranger with similar features to a loved one, or thinking about what you were doing this time a month or a year ago can also be triggers. While the triggers may not always be obvious at first, once you can identify them you can be better prepared for them next time. What usually happens over time is that a wave's pick-up or recovery time becomes faster after these trigger waves hit (see figure 2.1). From the figure you can see that although the trigger wave peaks at a high intensity, the pattern then continues as it was – at a relatively low intensity – rather than returning to the intense waves found in the period immediately after the death. It is also common that the waves increase in intensity again as the first anniversary nears, where you might think that this time last year we were doing this or that. Usually after the first anniversary the waves subside and the pattern continues as before.

Grief can also follow a different pattern. As shown in figure 2.2, the individual waves may be quite flat at the beginning and peak over the course of the next few months when the reality of the death starts to sink in.

Figure 2.3 shows a third pattern where there is little variation in the intensity of the waves as time goes on.

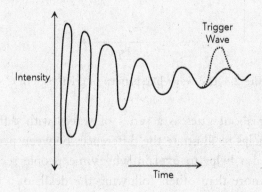

Figure 2.1 The wave-like pattern of grief, pattern A

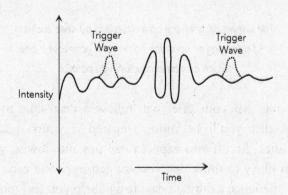

Figure 2.2 The wave-like pattern of grief, pattern B

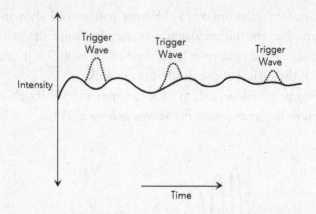

Figure 2.3 The wave-like pattern of grief, pattern C

Thinking about grief as a series of waves with different triggers helps to illustrate the differences between people's grief. It also helps to explain why some people seem to struggle more than others following the death of a loved one, and why grief can seem to intensify after a period of feeling better.

The waves of grief are characterised by deep sadness and a longing or yearning to be with your loved one, which can be excruciatingly painful.

Knowing that your grief will follow a wave-like pattern means that you'll be more prepared if yours suddenly intensifies. And if you expect these ups and downs, you'll be less likely to think that you are getting worse each time you experience a difficult day. It will help you feel more in control if you have an idea of what to expect, and this in turn will help your grieving process. It's also important to realise that no one else's grief will follow the same wave-like pattern as yours, because your experience and your triggers are unique. Some days will be better than others and you may feel as though your waves of grief are easing; other days will feel as though there is never a break from your grief. Exercise 2.1 will help you look at your own wave-like pattern of grief.

EXERCISE 2.1: YOUR WAVE-LIKE PATTERN OF GRIEF

What kind of ups and downs have you already encountered since the death of your loved one? In your journal, try to draw your wave-like pattern of grief. Can you identify any particular triggers that set off a more intense reaction? Can you identify any times where you felt as though things were a little easier? It might help to write some notes next to these peaks, to record your triggers and help you prepare for the next time one arises. Similarly, make a note of anything that helped to ease your pain.

You may have already heard the saying 'time heals all wounds'. Possibly a friend or relative has said these words to you, hoping that they will bring comfort. To some extent time does help, but it's more complicated than that. Imagine going to sleep today for three months, and then waking up again. The intensity of your pain would be the same then as it is today. It's not just the passage of time that helps ease grief's hold; it's what you do in that time that makes the difference. Even though your motivation and desire to do things might now be at an all-time low, it is important to just *do* things even if you don't feel like it. It's also important to begin to develop new routines, which will be discussed in Chapter 5.

It's not just the passage of time that helps; it's what
you do in that time that counts.

What you might experience

If you can understand more fully what you are experiencing, you might feel less alone and more likely to be able to gain a greater sense of control over your grief. Exercise 2.2 will help give you some idea about why you feel the way you do at the moment and why the simplest things seem so hard.

EXERCISE 2.2: WRITING WITH YOUR OTHER HAND

In your journal write your name and address with your non-dominant hand. Write as neatly as you can. Reflect on this process for a moment. How does your writing compare to when you write with your dominant hand? How did it feel? Did you have to concentrate more? Did it feel awkward or strange?

Imagine you were asked to complete this exercise every day for the next year. Would your writing improve? Yes. Would it be as neat and feel as comfortable as with your dominant hand? Probably not.

You might be wondering why you were asked to do this exercise. The reason is that it helps people understand why they feel the way they do when they are grieving. There is something familiar yet unfamiliar about writing with your other hand. You know how to attempt the task but it feels strange. The same applies to living your life after a loved one has died. Even though you know how to live, your life feels awkward and unfamiliar. It takes more concentration and energy and you might even feel like giving up.

From a psychological perspective, grief is made up of loss and change. Any change in a person's life, including positive changes such as marriage, result in a transition involving new learning and a period of adjustment. In the handwriting exercise the change is brought about by the 'loss' of your dominant hand for writing. Being able to write effectively with your other hand would require a lot of practice and a period of adjustment. Even after many years of experience, writing with your non-dominant hand may never feel as effortless as writing with your dominant hand.

Listed below are some of the thoughts and feelings that people experience soon after the death of a loved one.

WHAT TO EXPECT WHEN GRIEF IS NEW

- Difficulty concentrating
- Lethargy
- Tiredness
- Feeling fuzzy in the head
- Thinking you are going crazy or losing your mind
- Pining or yearning for your loved one
- Having little motivation
- Difficulty learning new information
- Difficulty in making decisions
- Being unable to control your emotions
- Feeling less tolerant of others
- Crying easily
- Anxiety
- A desire to be alone
- Not wanting to be alone
- Having dreams or nightmares about death and dying
- Entertaining thoughts of dying so that you can be with your loved one

Another good example that highlights how grief affects your day-to-day life is the experience of driving in a foreign country on the opposite side of the road. If you've ever done this, even if you have been driving for years, it's unnerving and requires a great deal of concentration and energy. Over time you would adapt and after a number of years it would probably feel relatively normal. But it would take a lot of time and practice to feel confident in an emergency situation.

Grief is made up of loss and change, which involves new learning and a period of adjustment.

PINING OR YEARNING

Pining or yearning for a loved one after they have died is believed to be one of the main features of grief that distinguishes it from depression. According to the dictionary, *to pine* means 'to suffer with longing or long painfully'. *To yearn* is defined as 'having an earnest or strong desire; to long'. Many people who are grieving describe this intense feeling of pining or yearning as excruciatingly painful. They have been separated from someone they love, and even though they know at all levels of their being that they will never see them again in this life, they tend to search or scan their environment hoping to find them. In much the same way as a fever is the body's way of combating an infection, it seems as though pining or yearning is the brain and heart's way of coming to terms with the loss of a loved one.

Gradually, as the bereaved person gets used to the absence of their loved one, the intensity of their pining or yearning lessens.

> *I was devastated when he was killed. It was such a shock. After the funeral, when things started to settle down, I remember being aware of this tremendous ache. It's hard to describe it but I really missed him and longed to see him again. I was pining for him, like a dog whimpering for his master to return home. That feeling has left me now but it is what I remember most about those early months.*
>
> HAZEL, 58

EXPECTATIONS ABOUT GRIEF

It's been six weeks and I thought I'd be better by now. It's common to hear people say something like this, but it's nearly impossible to anticipate how you will react when someone you love dies. It's one of those things, like giving birth or recovering from major surgery, that you won't know what it feels like – regardless of how much preparation you've done beforehand – until you've actually experienced it.

Your expectations play a huge role in your experience of grief and how you view your 'progress'. Put simply an 'expectation' is the mindset you have about the way you think something *will* be. We have expectations about everything in life, including our relationships, our work and our friends. We also have expectations about grief and how we *think* we should feel. Problems arise when there is a difference between how we thought we would be (the expectation) and how we actually are (the reality).

An expectation is a mindset you have about the way you think something will be.

Depending on how long ago your loved one died, you might be questioning your progress and wondering whether your experience is 'normal'. Two of the most common 'complaints' people express when they are grieving are, *I shouldn't still be crying,* and, *I thought I'd be better by now.* Both statements involve unrealistic expectations about progress that are perpetuated by the fast-paced society in which we live. Too often people expect that coming to terms with the death of a loved one will be a linear process without any hiccups along the way. In other words they think, *The more time that goes by, the better I will feel* (see figure 2.4). If you tend to think this way, it is far more realistic to see grief in terms of the wave-like pattern, as shown in figures 2.1, 2.2 and 2.3. Not only are these patterns a realistic representation of the ups and downs people experience when they are grieving, but they demonstrate how everyone's grief is unique.

Unfortunately in today's world we have come to expect things to happen almost immediately. We send an email and expect a reply within hours; we heat a frozen meal in a microwave and it's ready to eat in minutes; and we visit the doctor expecting to leave with a prescription to 'cure' our ailments. Our world is fast: it is technology driven and there is little patience. It's no wonder that some people

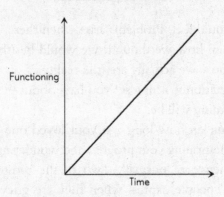

Figure 2.4 Unrealistic expectations about progress

think they should have stopped crying within days and be 'better' within weeks.

Grief does not operate by these same rules. In fact it has a life of its own – it knows no rules, time limits or pressures. Grief cannot be hurried. Understanding that you need to be patient with yourself when you are dealing with the death of a loved one is one of the first steps to overcoming grief. Giving yourself permission to be sad is another important initial step. If you don't allow yourself to feel your pain, you are really denying yourself the opportunity to properly grieve the death of your loved one.

Exercise 2.3 lists a number of unrealistic and unhelpful beliefs commonly expressed about people who are grieving.

Which ones have you heard? And which ones do you believe yourself?

EXERCISE 2.3: UNHELPFUL BELIEFS ABOUT BEREAVED PEOPLE

Step 1. Tick any of the unhelpful beliefs listed below that someone has said to you or that you have said to yourself.

Step 2. List any other unhelpful beliefs you have heard.

Step 3. Circle those that you believe to be true.

Step 4. Spend five minutes reflecting on any of the beliefs you've circled, and note down in your journal anything that comes to mind.

Beliefs expressed by others	Beliefs expressed by bereaved people
You've got to get on with your life	I've got to snap out of it
You've got to get over it	I've got to get over it
You've got to be strong	I thought I was strong
You've got to stop crying	I've got to stop crying
You've got to think of the children	I've got to put on a brave front for the children
You should be better by now	I should be better by now
_____	_____
_____	_____
_____	_____
_____	_____
_____	_____
_____	_____

Sad doesn't mean bad

Western society has programmed us to believe that showing strong emotion is a character weakness, when in fact it is simply a normal human response. In the case of grief you have to tell yourself that feeling sad isn't negative or a sign of weakness. In fact feelings of deep sadness are an expected reaction to the loss of someone you truly loved. If you can tell yourself that feeling sad is 'normal' then you will be less likely to put pressure on yourself to stop crying and about not yet being 'better'. It's important to realise that feeling sad can also be a reaction to the death of someone where the relationship was strained or had a history of problems.

Apart from interpreting crying as a sign of weakness, what people also find difficult about crying is that they have little control over their tears. Soon after a death you might find it almost impossible to go for long periods without crying, or your tears may catch you off guard. You might be at home and think about something and start crying. You might be out trying to finalise something and all of a sudden you burst into tears.

> *I had gone to the bank to take my husband's name off our account. When the teller said hello, I felt the tears well up and I wanted to run. I felt so stupid but she was very understanding.*
>
> JANET, 61

As hard as it is, allow yourself to feel sad and to cry. These are normal responses to losses of any kind. Crying is one way of releasing the build-up of pain when you are griev-ing. In fact research shows that crying helps rid the body of stress-induced chemicals, which is why most people say they feel better after having a good cry. Don't be afraid to let it happen. Don't fight it – crying is good for you.

> *Crying is good for you as it's the body's way of releas-ing stress-induced chemicals.*

Even though you might feel very vulnerable at the moment, you need to make sure that you don't fall into the trap of thinking your grief should be over by now. A number of realistic beliefs about grief and what to expect are listed below. Compare these to the unhelpful beliefs listed in exercise 2.3.

REALISTIC BELIEFS ABOUT GRIEF AND BEREAVED PEOPLE

- Grief cannot be hurried
- There is no quick fix for grief
- Grief is not an illness with a prescribed cure
- Grieving is healthy as it gives you the time to adjust to life without your loved one
- If you loved deeply, you cannot expect to grieve shallowly
- Crying is one way to express grief
- It is normal to feel very sad when someone you love dies

- Grief follows a wave-like pattern with ups and downs
- There is no right way to grieve
- Until you've reached the first anniversary of the death, many of the triggers to your grief remain unknown
- Children benefit from learning that grief is a normal reaction to loss

If your thinking tends to be unrealistic at times – more like the beliefs in exercise 2.3 than those in the list above – it might be more helpful to tell yourself these two things periodically.

- It's unrealistic to think that I can just get over the death of my loved one in a matter of weeks or months
- Expressing my pain doesn't mean I am weak. In fact it is one way to help me come to terms with their death and to begin to take control of my grief

Grief isn't over in an instant

If you are reading this book because someone you loved has recently died then, as hard as it is to hear, expect your feelings of sadness and longing to continue for some months to come. In time your waves of grief will lessen in intensity and frequency, and things will get easier. Expect to have a mixture of good and bad days for at least the first year.

Hopefully, as the year goes on, you will have more good days than bad days. Thinking that there will be good and bad days for at least the first year or two sets the expectation that it is normal to have down days, even after periods of feeling as though you have been doing better. Hopefully there will be fewer bad days in the second year, fewer again in the third, and so on. Healthy grieving involves getting through all the firsts: holidays, birthdays, significant dates and the first anniversary of your loved one's death. Remember that there is no magic cure for grief. There is no quick fix.

As you read on you will learn strategies that can help you overcome the hold grief has on you. These strategies or tools will not only help you get through each day, but will help you regain some sense of control in your life. Unfortunately there is no 'on/off' switch to grief. But by using these strategies you can turn your grief down in much the same way as you'd turn down the volume on a stereo. Remember that everyone's grief is different, and what will help you feel more in control is giving yourself permission to take the time you need to grieve.

SUGGESTION: 'VOLUME CONTROL'

It is far more realistic to think of grief as having a volume control rather than an 'on/off' switch. In the early months when your grief is new, aim to do things that help you turn down the volume of your grief little by little.

Summary

- Grieving gives you the time and space to adjust to life without your loved one
- Loss and change are two important components of grief
- Grief runs its own course
- Sad doesn't mean bad
- Grief isn't over in an instant

3

Permission
to grieve

Giving yourself permission to grieve the death of someone you loved is essential if you want to overcome your grief to the point that you can enjoy your life again. But what does this actually involve? It's important to understand that grieving does not mean 'getting over' their death or forgetting them, which many people fear. Rather, being able to grieve the death of your loved one in a healthy way means giving yourself the time and space to get used to them not being here anymore. You will always miss them and notice the void in your life, but eventually you will overcome the raw physical and emotional pain that is your grief. Giving yourself permission to grieve involves telling yourself that it is normal to be sad, that it is perfectly acceptable to ask difficult questions, and totally understandable to express your concerns about your future. This chapter will help you to start thinking about how you might be able to express your grief in a number of different ways.

Death brings change

Many things change in your life when someone close to you dies. This is inevitable. How much your life changes correlates with how closely your lives overlapped, and the impact the death of your loved one has on your future. Maybe you had been married or in a relationship with them for a long time, or had cared for them for the years they were ill. Maybe now you have to move house or return to work. Changes associated with the death of your loved one can often make the grieving process much more difficult. At a time when you are struggling with adjusting to the absence of your loved one, you could find yourself faced with many problems that you didn't have before.

> *My husband was still working when he became sick early in the summer. Neither of us expected him to die — we thought he was going to get better. I had stopped working a few years ago and we were looking forward to his retirement. My husband and I did everything together. Now I just don't know what I'm going to do. He's left me in such a mess and I just don't know where to begin. I can't manage the house, I no longer have health insurance, and without his income I think I will have to sell. I wish I'd been the one to go first. He would have known what to do.*
>
> DEBORAH, 57

Thinking of grief in terms of change is helpful in understanding why you may feel overwhelmed at first, and why it's important to be patient with yourself. It might also help those who are supporting you to gain a better idea about the complexity of grief and understand why it is not over in an instant. As outlined in Chapter 2, death results in both loss and change, which requires a period of new learning and adjustment. That's why being able to take the time to grieve is so crucial. Grieving gives you the space you need to adjust slowly to new roles and different situations. It is a necessary part of learning to live without a loved one. It also gives you time to re-evaluate your beliefs and assumptions about how you expected your life to be.

> *It's very difficult for me now. What my family doesn't realise is that I went from my parents' home to my husband's. I was married when I was 18 years old. I'm now 79. He took care of our finances and I took care of our home. I'm now having to learn things that I've never worried about before.*
>
> BEATRICE, 79

> *My whole world changed when my 11-year-old son died under tragic circumstances. So much of my life was centred on his sporting activities – there was such a void on so many levels after his death.*
>
> SIENNA, 33

Grieving gives you the space you need to adjust slowly to new roles and different situations. It also gives you the time to reconcile how your life is now different from the way you expected it to be.

Healthy grieving

You might question whether grieving can ever be 'healthy' because it feels so horrible. But most of us will face the death of someone we love at some stage in our lives, and it is helpful to see dying as a part of life. If you can grieve openly and without limitations, eventually you will be able to move forward without your loved one. But to do this you have to pay attention to your grief and become an active participant in it, not a passive recipient.

It seems that people do better overall if they embrace their grief rather than fight it. Healthy grieving is about being able to take control of your grief rather than allowing your grief to take control of you. Accepting that your life has taken a turn in a different direction is one important component of overcoming your grief. The path your life is now on will be different to the life you were living when your loved one was alive. But before we look at this different path, let's look at why it is beneficial to express your grief in some way.

Remember, healthy grieving means becoming an active participant instead of a passive recipient.

Wound analogy

Grief needs to be expressed in one way or another, even though it is a painful process. Many people find the 'wound analogy' helpful in understanding why it is so important to express their grief.

Imagine you have a huge, infected wound on your leg that is causing you extreme pain and discomfort. It is deep and raw. Before it can begin to heal you need to get the 'gunk' or infection out. You may need antibiotic treatment or a daily dressing, and the wound will only start to heal over after the infection has gone. Over time the wound will become less tender and eventually you will be able to touch it without causing pain. But the wound remains marked by a scar and you will always be able to recall the pain that was associated with the injury and the infection.

Even though this is an unpleasant analogy, it demonstrates the need for you to express your grief if it is causing you distress. In the long run it won't help if you try to suppress your emotions or put on a brave front. In fact it is likely to make matters worse. Having said this, though, it's important to realise that there is no right way to grieve. Your grief is unique, so however you grieve is right for you. You might want to talk to others about your pain and loss, or you may be a very private person and want to keep it to yourself. Neither way is better than the other. It is up to you to work out what is best for you.

There is no right way to grieve. It is up to you to work out how best to express your grief.

Grief is complex

Grief is comprised of many different layers relating to loss. Contrary to popular opinion, grief is not a single entity that you can just cure or fix. It is not like having an ear infection that, once treated, goes away and your hearing 'returns to normal'. When someone you love dies, your life changes forever. Not only are you grieving the loss of the person, but you are grieving the loss of the life you had with them and your hopes and dreams for the future. As a result of their death you are likely to experience many different losses that result in change. It's important to acknowledge that, if your loved one had been ill for some time, you may have experienced a number of losses before their death as their health deteriorated.

Being able to adjust to the changes you now face takes time, especially if there is a lot of emotion involved. When emotion runs high, irrespective of the issue at hand, your ability to think clearly is compromised. When you are grieving, things that were once simple may now seem very difficult and require much more of your energy and concentration – just as if you were driving on the other side of the road in a foreign country. If you think of grief as being complex and multifaceted, you will be more likely to be patient with yourself and resist the urge to say, *I should be over this by now.*

SUGGESTION: ACKNOWLEDGING YOUR
LOSSES

If your loved one was ill for some time before they
died, it is important to acknowledge that you may
have lost many things prior to their death as their
health deteriorated. It's important that you acknowledge these losses too, not just those that came after
your loved one died.

What have you lost?

When someone dies, we know intellectually that our contact with them ceases on the day they die, which is heart-
wrenching. We can no longer interact with them at any
physical or verbal level. Coming to terms with this loss is a
huge task and it may seem impossible. There will never be
another kiss, hug or conversation. If the death was expected,
you might have prepared for this in some way and had a
chance to give that last hug or kiss. But if their death was
unexpected you will have had no time to prepare.

With death we naturally focus on 'who' died. But with
any death comes the loss of so many other things – not
just 'who' they were to you. In losing your loved one, you
might also lose your best friend, your partner, your confidant, your mentor or the person who looked after the odd
jobs around the house. You may lose your financial advisor,

problem-solver or sounding board. Being able to identify what you've lost is important because it relates to the complexity of your grief. By identifying the roles that your loved one played in your life, you can work out where else you need to focus your attention and ask for support as you begin to take control of your grief. Other losses you may feel are the roles you played in their life, like in George's case.

> *My wife had been ill for several years with amyotrophic lateral sclerosis (ALS), a degenerative neurological disease. She was the love of my life and we were always together. As her illness progressed I was her sole caregiver. Looking after her became my job. I rarely left her side except for when one of our children came over so that I could do what needed to be done. After she died, one of the hardest things was working out how to fill my days. I had lost my job as well as the love of my life.*

> GEORGE, 68

Exercise 3.1 will help you identify these roles. Once you've done this, you will be able to see why grief is far more complex than is often believed, and why it is unrealistic for you or anyone around you to expect that it will be over in an instant. Adjusting to life without your loved one means addressing all these other losses. It's likely that some of the things your loved one provided cannot be replaced, nor should you expect them to be. But other things can be, and exploring what the alternatives are will help you feel more in control.

EXERCISE 3.1: WHAT HAVE YOU LOST?

Listed below are some of the roles your loved one may have played in your life – or perhaps you played in theirs. Tick off any that you have 'lost' with the death of your loved one. If you can think of others, list them too.

Partner	Friend
Confidant	Teacher
Sexual partner	Companion
Financial advisor	Sounding board
Chef	Handy-person
House cleaner	Gardener
Mentor	Sparring partner
Coach	My greatest fan
Hopes for future	Travelling companion
Dreams for future	Sense of safety
Comedian	Life of the party
Social organiser	House manager
Mechanic	Bill payer
Taxi driver	Child manager
Shared history	Financial security
Parent of my child	Last call of the night
My caring role	Independence
Lost opportunities	Other _____
	_____
	_____
	_____

When our only child died at 19 in an accident, our lives changed forever. With his death we lost our son and all our hopes and dreams – his graduation from college, marriage and maybe one day grandchildren. It felt as though we weren't even parents anymore.

MICHELLE, 50

After my husband died it took me a while to realise that with his death, the one thing I had lost that I treasured was that I was always his last call of the day. He travelled a lot for work and whenever he was away, he would always call me and we would speak before bed. It's hard to describe how much I miss that call and what it represents – it can't be replaced.

JOAN, 55

SUGGESTION: LOSING YOUR SEXUAL PARTNER

Having an intimate sexual relationship is an important part of most marriages or long-term relationships. When one partner dies, the sexual relationship that was shared between the two no longer exists. Like many aspects of grief, the loss of a sexual relationship, its history and the intimacy that accompanies that, is rarely discussed. Being able to grieve this loss as part of your other losses is important in overcoming your grief. One way to do this is to find someone you feel comfortable with, and with whom you can express your feelings about this loss and how it relates to your overall loss. If you have no one to confide in, you might find it helpful to speak to a counsellor or to write your thoughts in your journal. Sometimes you just need to be able to acknowledge these losses to yourself.

My world was shattered when my fiancé died. We had been together for four years and were planning to get married in the spring. He was killed in a freak boating accident and apparently died instantly. I never had a chance to say goodbye and to tell him how much I loved him. We had met when I was 34 years old, and he had a child from his first marriage. Part of my struggle now, a year later, is realising that not only did I lose my best friend who was always there for me, but I've lost my chance of having the family I've always wanted. Now my friends are telling me I need to start dating again, but I'm so sad and heartbroken – at 38 it's the last thing I want to do.

FIONA, 38

Depending on how recently your loved one died, exercise 3.1 may have been very painful to complete. Often people say that the reality of their loved one's death really started to sink in when they realised what else they had lost. In a way you need to grieve each loss separately. For example, a major part of Fiona's heartache was coming to terms with the fact that there was a very real possibility she would never have children and the family she had always hoped for. Similarly Geraldine, who tells her story next, struggled after she had a miscarriage during a much wanted pregnancy.

> *We had tried to become pregnant for years without success. After several IVF attempts I gave up because it was just too hard, both emotionally and physically. Then without trying I found out I was pregnant – finally. I was ecstatic, only to be devastated when I had a miscarriage at five months. I've lost all hope now that I will ever be able to have my own child. This thought never leaves me.*
>
> GERALDINE, 35

Express your pain

There are no specific rules or guidelines about how to express your grief, but most people say that they feel better when they let their grief out in some way. There are many ways to do this such as crying, talking, exercising, keeping a journal, attending a support group, thinking through difficult issues and being creative. Being able to tell your story helps you to express your grief. This is not just for those of you who had wonderful relationships. Reconciling difficult relationships is also a part of grieving. Maybe your relationship with the person who died was full of heart-ache and sorrow. Maybe you were waiting for things to get better. Whatever your relationship was, grief is better out than in. And in letting it out it's important to take the time to respect your grief, which involves acknowledging and expressing your thoughts and feelings about your loss. If you keep your emotions pent up inside, the danger is that you can compromise your physical and psychological well-being.

It's important to respect your grief by acknowledging your thoughts and feelings.

Carve out 'grief time'

Like any worthwhile task it's important to 'carve out' time from your day to grieve, even if it means scheduling it into your calendar. If you don't make time you can become so consumed with the busyness of life that you risk placing your grief on the back burner. People with hectic careers, or the parents of young children, for example, can find themselves in this situation. Allowing their grief to be pushed aside by these demands is not intentional – it just happens.

Scheduling 'grief time' in your day will help you feel a greater sense of control.

You might be wondering whether you will feel like your old self ever again. Planning a specific time of the day to sit down and give yourself time to think about the death of your loved one, allows you to express your grief in a contained way. This will help you feel more in control if you feel overwhelmed or consumed by your grief. One way to carve out this grief time is to allocate twenty to thirty minutes each day, or every other day, to thinking about your loved one. Plan a time of day when you won't be interrupted and don't have to rush off immediately after you have finished. You can allocate longer if you choose to. Exercise 3.2 outlines suggestions for what to do in your grief time.

EXERCISE 3.2 CARVING OUT AND STRUCTURING YOUR 'GRIEF TIME'

Allocate twenty to thirty minutes each day or every other day to focus on your grief. Below are some suggestions about what you could do during your 'grief time'. Choose the ones that appeal to you the most.

- Sit quietly, close your eyes and think about your loved one
- Play music that reminds you of your loved one
- Talk to him or her about your day, as though they were sitting next to you
- Allow yourself to cry – remember that sad doesn't mean bad

- Write in your journal – see Appendix 1 for suggestions on how to start
- Write your loved one a letter
- Write about the events surrounding their death
- List the things you miss about him or her
- List any questions you have – see Chapter 4
- Look through photographs of your time together
- Make a list about what needs to be done – see Chapter 4
- Find a creative outlet such as poetry, painting, gardening or music
- Make a memory or photo book that tells their story – see Chapter 7
- Find a quiet and comforting place outdoors, where you can think about your loved one and reflect on your life together

By scheduling time in this way, you are containing or compartmentalising your grief. Although it may be painful to focus on your grief like this, many people report that they actually feel 'better' when they do set time aside, because they feel more able to get on with the rest of their day. It also sends a clear message to your brain that grieving is important and you are not neglecting your feelings. In time you'll find that you probably won't feel the need to carve out as much time to grieve. In the next few chapters you will find other suggestions and exercises about what to do in your 'grief time'.

Carving out grief time sends a clear message to your brain that grieving is important.

I wrote in a journal nearly every day for the first six months or so after my husband died. It really helped me sort through all the different thoughts and feelings I was having. As time went on, I wrote less often and that felt okay. I saw it as a sign that my life was getting easier again. Now, three years later, I write on his birthday, the anniversary of his death and when I have something special to tell him.

GEORGIA, 52

About five months after my daughter died, I went to see a grief counsellor because I felt as though I was getting worse. She suggested that I set aside twenty minutes each morning to focus on my grief. For me this was very helpful — I told myself that when the time was up I needed to go about what I had to do for the day. If I hadn't structured it this way, I think my grief would have spilled over into my whole day and I don't think I would have managed all the other things I needed to take care of.

CAROLE, 55

SUGGESTION: FOR COUPLES WHO ARE GRIEVING

If two of you are grieving the same loss, as with the death of a child, then how you grieve will depend a lot on the type of person you are and how you react in difficult or emotional situations. Because men and women often express their emotions differently, try not to make comparisons between the ways in which each of you is grieving. This is especially important if one of you is more focused on completing tasks and the other is more focused on being able to express their pain. Avoid criticisms or judgements. Being able to share your thoughts and feelings will help you feel more aligned, even if you are grieving in different ways. If you need your space, let your partner know, so they don't take your actions personally. It's easy to fall into the trap of thinking you might make the other person upset if you bring up the subject of the death of your loved one. Even though this is a commonly expressed fear, most people say they are always thinking about their loved one at some level, and that there is nothing that could make them sadder. Try to check in with each other on a regular basis about your thoughts and feelings – it might help you feel stronger and more united as a couple. If you find it difficult to talk to each other on your own, you could benefit from seeing a grief counsellor together who can help you share your thoughts and feelings in a constructive way.

Writing to your loved one

As they grieve their loss, many people find it very helpful to write to their loved one on a regular basis. The advantage of writing down your thoughts and feelings is that it takes much more cognitive processing to put down your ideas on paper than to just think them through. If something is troubling you, writing about it is a great way to try to make sense of it. If you are using a journal for completing the exercises in *Overcoming Grief*, you could use the same journal for your letters. Alternatively, you might want to use a separate journal so the letters are all in the same place. Exercise 3.3 lists some ideas about how to start, and there are more suggestions in Appendix 1. It's a good idea to date each entry or letter so you can keep track of what you were thinking and feeling at different times.

EXERCISE 3.3 WRITING TO YOUR LOVED ONE

Writing can be a wonderful way to express your grief, and at the same time it maintains a connection to your loved one. Write in your journal whenever you feel like it. You can write as a part of your 'grief time' or you can write whenever you feel the need to connect with your loved one. Maybe it's to tell them about the day's events or to ask their advice; or maybe it's just to express your thoughts and feelings. Below are a few suggestions about ways to get started. Remember always to make a note of the date. This way you can keep a record of how you were feeling on a given day and look back over your progress.

- It's been___days/weeks/months since you've been gone and I wanted to tell you how I've been getting on.
- If you were here today I would tell you . . .
- Before you died I wish I'd had the chance to tell you . . .
- I'm concerned about . . . I want to know what your advice would be. I think you would say . . .
- I wanted to tell you about what I've been doing . . .

Here is an example of what someone might write. After Lauren's father died she started to keep a journal; these are extracts from different points in time.

This is my first entry. I have decided to keep this journal for two reasons: to help me come to terms with dad's death; and to have a record of my memories and thoughts, which one day I can show to dad's grandchildren. Yesterday was five weeks to the day since his death. I still cannot believe it, although I do 'know' it. It is so difficult to understand the exact reasons why he died so young, seemingly so fit and healthy. I miss him terribly; his jovial way and silly jokes . . .

Eleven weeks today. On one hand time seems to be going fast, but on the other, slow. I still find it hard to believe that 'dad is dead'. I know he is, but it's also hard not to think he's just at home with mum. I miss his phone calls. I fear not being able to remember the exact sound of his voice . . .

It's been four months today since dad died. I suppose this month has been a little easier than last month. I don't think a day has yet gone by when I haven't discussed dad with someone or thought about him . . .

His first anniversary is a few days away. This time last year he was in hospital having some tests. Oh – to be able to turn back the clock. Nearly a year has passed – no new memories of dad this year. I fear losing his image in my brain and the sound of his voice.

Now it's a year later – time has flown. Tonight we fly out to the USA – something to take my mind off today and the next few days. The anniversary of his funeral is also on my mind. I want next week to come: not to shut dad out – he is always foremost in my mind – but to shut out the pain of this time last year. The emotional energy expended is now beyond my imagination. I couldn't go through it again. I will spend some time today – about the

*time dad died – in a beautiful church and walking through
the botanical gardens. Hopefully they will be open . . .*

EXTRACTS FROM LAUREN'S JOURNAL

A different path – not of your choosing

Life is commonly referred to as a journey. If you think in
these terms, then before your loved one died you were
travelling together on one path irrespective of the nature of
your relationship. Most people have a sense of where they
are heading on their path. Unfortunately with the death
of your loved one, you come to a fork in your path. At
the fork you're forced onto a different path heading off in
another direction. This new path is not one of your choosing and you're unsure of what lies ahead. The path you
were on originally is closed and now no longer an option.
The challenge you now face, which we'll discuss in more
detail in Chapter 9, is finding out how to make this new
path as rewarding as possible given that you wished that you
were still on your original path. Before you can do this, you
need to pay attention to your grief and work out what you
have to do to express your loss, and how to help yourself
adjust to living without your loved one.

It's up to you

It would be nice if we could delegate or outsource our grief
so that someone else could deal with it. But it's impossible

to love someone deeply and not grieve at all. Ironically, at a time when you are feeling most vulnerable, you are the only one who truly knows what you need – even though it might take you some time to work it out. You need to speak up for what you can and can't do, because there will be many people who will want to tell you how you *should* be feeling and what you *should* be doing. Even though they might be very well intentioned, a lot of what they suggest will not be helpful or realistic. It's also likely that you will be disappointed or hurt at times by people's behaviour, especially if they don't act in the way you thought they would. It would be wonderful if people knew instinctively how to help, but they don't. You need to take the lead by asking for help and showing them how to help you grieve.

At times you will need to remind yourself, and those around you, that grief has a life of its own and it cannot be hurried. Grieving in a healthy way involves working through your thoughts and feelings not only about the death of your loved one, but also about your life without them. It may involve telling your story over and over again. It might require lots of soul-searching in an attempt to answer difficult questions, or it simply may mean lots of hard work as you struggle to find meaning in your life. Even though there is no right way to grieve, grieving does require you to take action. What this action is will be different for everyone, and you may have to try a few things before you find the right one for you.

You need to be your best advocate.

SUGGESTION: USEFUL REMINDERS WHEN YOU ARE GRIEVING

Remember that no one else:

- can feel your pain
- can take away your pain
- knows how you are feeling
- knows what you need

Accept that:

- people can be well meaning but sometimes misguided in what they say
- many people won't know what to say to comfort you
- some people will appear intolerant and tell you to 'get over it'
- you can't always count on the people you thought you could
- you will need to speak up for yourself about what is best for you

Summary

- You need to give yourself permission to grieve the death of your loved one
- Grieving does not mean forgetting your loved one
- Healthy grieving requires you to become an active participant in your grief
- When someone dies there are many losses associated with their death
- Grief is complex and multifaceted
- Grief cannot be outsourced
- You need to speak up about what you need

4

Regaining control

As weeks turn into months, the reality of your loved one's death will begin to sink in slowly. You know that they are not coming back and that your life has changed, and your emotions will continue to follow the wave-like pattern discussed in Chapter 2. Eventually you will get to the point where you know deep down that you have to do something to regain a sense of control in your life. Some people refer to this as 'turning the corner'.

> *My husband had been dead for six months and I wasn't taking care of myself. I was drinking too much and I knew I had to do something when I nearly drove off the road one night. That's when I went for grief counselling.*
>
> JENNIFER, 57

Jennifer could pinpoint the time when she realised that she needed to do something different, and made a conscious decision to take action. That didn't mean she felt less pain, but it did mean that she was prepared to begin to put things in place to help get her life back on track. Making the decision to tackle her grief was the first step. Jennifer's case might seem extreme – it may be that all it takes for you is to wake up one day and realise that you need to do something different. You might realise that you can't continue as you are – that you need to do something to help yourself. The next two chapters will outline a number of strategies that target your thoughts and behaviour following the death of your loved one. Working through these exercises will help you begin to take control again in your life and lessen the hold grief has on you.

Compartmentalising your worries

It can feel overwhelming when someone you love dies – there are so many things that need to be done apart from dealing with your loss and the ways in which your life has changed. The amount of control you currently feel you have will depend on how easily you have been able to work through troubling issues. Regaining a sense of control will help your waves of grief lessen in intensity and frequency, as outlined in Chapter 2. But knowing what to do to feel more in control might be more difficult than it appears. Often people realise that they have little control, but rarely do they know instinctively what they need to do to increase their sense of control. Finalising legal and financial affairs adds another layer of complexity and is particularly troubling for most people, especially if they're not used to dealing with these matters.

Exercise 4.1 will help you prioritise what you need to do, while at the same time increasing your sense of control.

It involves imagining that you have a number of different boxes that you can fill with your worries.

EXERCISE 4.1: FILL YOUR WORRY BOXES

Step 1.   Make a list of the issues that are worrying you right now.

Step 2.   Group these issues into different categories.

Step 3.   Write a label that defines each of the groups you made in Step 2. For example, finances, house, children, work and so on.

Step 4.   Now imagine that you can take each group of issues and store them in a box. Each box has a lid that you can close.

Step 5.   Within each box, sort the issues in order of priority. What needs to be attended to now and what can wait? Place an asterisk next to the items that you want to address first.

While this might seem like a simple exercise, what you have done is to compartmentalise the many issues you are facing. Thinking about these issues all at once is daunting and far too much for anyone to solve. Once you've organised your issues into different boxes, it's much easier to look at the separate issues within each box and decide which ones you need to deal with immediately and which ones can wait. Listing and prioritising them this way takes more cognitive processing than just thinking about them. Remember how writing to your loved one in Chapter 3 helped to make sense of your thoughts? This works in the same way. And having your issues written down in categories allows you to add to them as you think of other things that need to be done.

Consider Donna, 52, whose husband Tom died suddenly six weeks ago. She felt she wasn't coping at all and was overwhelmed by what lay ahead. When Donna completed the 'Fill your worry boxes' exercise, her list in step 1 looked like this.

Step 1. Make a list of the issues that are worrying you right now.

- General finances
- Children's education
- Paying the mortgage
- Replying to sympathy cards
- Feeling cheated
- Selling Tom's car
- Finalising the will
- Changing our bank account details
- Upkeep of an old house
- Talking to the children about life without their father
- Deciding when to return to work
- Being alone at 52
- Needing to find a better-paid job
- Sorting through Tom's things

As Donna continued to work through the steps, she grouped her worries into finances/legal issues, children, house/personal, job and her future. She was able to prioritise what needed to be done first and decided to finalise her husband's will and see her bank manager to change the account details. She also arranged to meet up with her children who were away at university to talk openly to them about their future. Donna realised she would eventually have to consider changing jobs, but decided it was in her best interests to return to her current job where she knew exactly what it entailed.

Step 2. Group these issues into different categories.
Step 3. Write a label that defines each of the groups you made in step 2.
Step 5. *Indicates the issues Donna decided to attend to first.

Finances/legal issues
• General finances
• Paying the mortgage
• Changing bank accounts*
• Finalising the will*

Children
• Children's education
• Talking to the children about life without their father*

Job
- Deciding when to return to work
- Finding a better-paid job

Future
- Feeling cheated
- Being alone at 52

House/personal
- Upkeep of an old house
- Selling Tom's car
- Replying to sympathy cards*
- Sorting through Tom's things

Even though Donna still had many big decisions to make, she felt less overwhelmed after she had organised her worries in this way. She realised she didn't need to do everything immediately – sorting and prioritising what needed to be done made it much easier to develop a daily plan. And she gained a greater sense of control from the mental technique of imagining that she could close the lids on her boxes of worries.

SUGGESTION: SYMPATHY CARDS

If you want to respond to sympathy cards, sort them according to those you wish to (i) send a thank you card only; (ii) have another family member respond on your behalf; (iii) write a personal note of thanks; and (iv) phone and thank them in person. Once you've done this, arrange the cards in each group in order of priority and decide how many you can deal with realistically in a day and who can help you.

Generate a daily 'to do' list

Once you have sorted your worries in this way, you'll find it easier to set about writing a daily 'to do' list. Writing a list of things that you need to do on any given day is an excellent way of improving your sense of control. It's important to keep your expectations low and list only two or three things you need to get done that day. You might need to make one phone call, or go to the supermarket or bank. The aim is to break down large tasks into smaller, achievable steps. As the weeks go by, it's likely you'll find that you can do more each day.

Donna wrote a to do list every day and included something from several different 'boxes'. Here are two examples of her lists.

MONDAY

- Call the lawyer to arrange an appointment to finalise the will
- Call the bank to arrange an appointment to change our bank account details
- Reply to ten sympathy cards

TUESDAY

- Call the children to arrange a time to meet to discuss their future
- Reply to ten sympathy cards

Even though this might not seem like a lot, grief can make the most simple of tasks seem overwhelming and zap you of your energy. Following on from Exercise 4.1 where you listed your worries, you can now begin to plan the things that need to be done. Exercise 4.2 will help you prioritise the tasks on your list. Use either a diary or calendar to plan each day to give you a record of what you have achieved. Cross off each task as you complete it, which in itself is very rewarding. Remember to take small steps and plan one day at a time. As you continue, your sense of control will increase.

EXERCISE 4.2: YOUR DAILY TO DO LIST

Using your calendar or diary, make a daily list of the tasks you need to complete.

Step 1.   Make a list of the things in your different worry boxes that you need to achieve over the next few weeks.

What items did you mark with an asterisk in exercise 4.1?

Step 2.   Circle the things that are most pressing.

Step 3.   Break down bigger tasks into smaller steps.

Step 4.   List two or three things that you believe you can do tomorrow from steps 2 or 3.

Step 5.   List another two or three things that you can do the next day, and so on.

Step 6.   Cross off the tasks on your list as you complete them.

Step 7.   If you think of any other tasks that weren't on your original list, add them to one of your worry boxes and follow the steps above.

SUGGESTION: DON'T THINK TOO FAR AHEAD IN THE FIRST FEW MONTHS

When your life has been turned upside down like this, it's easy to let your thoughts run wild. What will your life be like in a year or two's time? Will you ever be happy again? Thinking this way can be overwhelming and increases your feeling of being out of control. Don't think too far ahead. Focus on what needs to be done today or next week, and put aside for the moment thoughts about next year or the year after.

Identifying your barriers

Is there anything concerning the death of your loved one that is playing over and over in your mind? These issues might include guilt, anger, regret and unanswered questions, and are likely to become barriers to working through your grief. Holding the belief that *life should be fair* can also become a potential barrier to your grief. If you have a strong belief that we live in a just and fair world, this belief will be challenged when someone you love dies prematurely, especially if their death was unexpected. Being able to change the way you think will help you overcome your barriers.

Guilt is the emotion people experience when they think they have done something wrong, whether or not they actually have. It is a destructive emotion and the thoughts behind it need to be challenged. Heather described the guilt she felt surrounding her husband's death.

> *I knew he was getting close to the end as our hospice nurse had told me about the signs of approaching death. I hadn't left his side, except for when one of our friends was leaving after a visit and I walked her out to get a coffee. I was only gone for five minutes and in that time he died. I feel so guilty — I'd promised him I'd be with him to the end.*
>
> HEATHER, 62

Anger can also be a huge barrier to many people if it keeps you stuck, as in Paul's case.

> *My son was killed in a car accident that wasn't his fault. A drunk driver in another car swerved on to his side of the road and hit him. My son died instantly but the other driver basically walked away unscathed. Once the shock faded, all I could feel was anger. It has consumed me and I feel as though I can't move on.*
>
> PAUL, 59

Regret is an emotion that many people express at some level. Regret about things not said, regret about things never done, and regret about hopes for the future. When Lara's mother died, she regretted not having said 'I love you'.

My mother died suddenly. I knew she was ill but I didn't think it was life-threatening. I saw her four days before she died – if I had known that would be the last time, I would have said 'I love you' when I left for work, instead of goodbye. Even though she knew I loved her, I wish I had said it one last time.

LARA, 27

EXERCISE 4.3: IDENTIFY YOUR BARRIERS

Do you feel guilt, anger or regret about anything to do with the death of your loved one? If so, write it down in the space below.

I feel guilty because

_____

I feel angry because

_____

I regret that I

_____

Once you can identify the barriers that are keeping you stuck, it is far easier to tackle them. As outlined in Chapter

3, it is very important to be able to articulate your thoughts surrounding the death, especially those that are troubling you. Once you can express your thoughts, you can set about challenging them if they are unhelpful or unrealistic.

Challenging unhelpful thoughts

When you're grieving, especially in the early months, you are likely to have many thoughts that are not accurate or helpful. In all aspects of life, the way we think affects how we feel and behave. Grieving is no different, except that your thoughts may be more distorted because you are vulnerable and not thinking as clearly as usual. The thoughts we have on a daily basis tend to occur automatically and are linked to the way we feel. If we want to change the way we feel, we need to change the way we think, which is the basic premise of cognitive behavioural therapy.

Let's consider a non-grief example. John is driving to work during peak hour. The traffic has come to a standstill. He is instantly aware that he feels irritated. He is thinking: *I'm going to be late for work; this is useless.* He begins to dart in and out of the traffic, trying to find the quickest way through. His friend Stephen also uses the same route and is caught in the same traffic jam. He feels calm and decides to listen to his new playlist and remain in his lane. He is thinking: *I'm going to be late for work but there is nothing I can do about the traffic.*

You can see in this example that John and Stephen reacted very differently to the same situation because they thought very differently. We can record John's thoughts, feelings and behaviour in the following way.

A	B	C
Situation or trigger	**Unhelpful thoughts**	**Feelings (score/10)** **Behaviour**
Caught in peak hour traffic jam	*I'm going to be late for work; this is useless*	Irritation (9/10) Driving impatiently

John's thinking about the situation is unhelpful and is likely to cause him to have an accident if he continues to drive impatiently. If he wants to react more like Stephen, he needs to challenge his unhelpful thoughts by asking himself the following questions.

1. Where's the evidence for what I thought in (B)?
2. What are the alternatives to what I thought in (B)?
3. What is the likely effect on me of thinking in this way?
4. How would I advise a friend to think in the same situation?

John asked himself questions 2, 3 and 4, and from his answers he was able to generate more helpful thoughts, which are recorded in the next table in (D). By thinking in a more helpful way, John's feelings changed (E), which in turn meant his behaviour changed (E).

A	B	C	D	E
Situation or trigger	Unhelpful thoughts	Feelings (score/10) Behaviour	Helpful thoughts	New feelings (score/10) New behaviour
Caught in peak hour traffic jam	*I'm going to be late for work; this is useless*	Irritation (9/10) Driving impatiently	*I'm going to be late for work, but there's nothing I can do about it. I could have an accident if I continue to drive impatiently.*	Irritation (4/10) Remain in lane

Challenging your thinking in this way is based on looking at both the evidence and how you can think realistically about situations. Given the intensity of John's initial irritation in (C), it would be unrealistic to expect that by changing his thinking he could become instantly calm in (E). This would be considered wishful thinking. But by challenging his thoughts he was able to reduce the intensity of his irritation from 9/10 to 4/10, which was enough of a reduction to bring about a positive change in his behaviour.

Record your thoughts

Changing the way you think takes practice. Psychologists encourage people to record or monitor their thoughts whenever they experience a strong negative reaction to a situation or event. This technique can be effective for many different problems including depression, anxiety and low self-esteem. And it lends itself very readily to challenging the unhelpful thoughts that people might have when they are grieving. The framework for challenging unhelpful thoughts – shown in exercise 4.4 – simplifies this process by using a 'thought diary' format. Note the extra question asking specifically about what your loved one would say to you if they were here now. This has been added to the list of questions to challenge your thinking.

EXERCISE 4.4: FRAMEWORK FOR CHALLENGING UNHELPFUL THOUGHTS

This framework can be used to help you challenge any unhelpful thoughts that are causing strong, negative emotions and/or destructive behaviour. Whenever you experience a negative emotion, use the thought diary format to challenge your thinking and generate new, helpful thoughts, which in turn will help change the way you feel. You will find a blank thought diary form in Appendix 2.

THOUGHT DIARY FORMAT

A	B	C	D	E
Situation or trigger	Unhelpful thoughts	Feelings (score/10) Behaviour	Helpful thoughts	New feelings (score/10) New behaviour

Step 1. Write down the situation, event or trigger in (A). It may be a memory of an event.

Step 2. Identify the main feeling or emotion you're experiencing and record this in (C) along with any unhelpful behaviours you've noticed. Rate the intensity of your feeling or emotion on a scale of 0–10, with 10 being the greatest or the strongest.

Step 3. Articulate the thought behind this feeling or emotion and record it in (B).

Step 4. Challenge your unhelpful thoughts using these five questions.

    1. Where's the evidence for what I thought in (B)?

    2. What are the alternatives to what I thought in (B)?

3. What is the likely effect on me of thinking in this way?

4. How would I advise a friend to think in the same situation?

5. What would my loved one tell me to do if they were here now?

Step 5. Rewrite your new, helpful thoughts in (D) using your answers to these questions.

Step 6. Identify the new feeling or emotion. Rate the intensity of your new emotion on a scale of 0–10 as you did in step 2. If you recorded a behaviour in (C), is there now a new behaviour that is constructive? In (E) record your new feeling and its rating, along with your new behaviour.

Now we can use this framework to consider an example about grief.

Guilt

Peggy, Jack's wife of forty-four years, was dying from pancreatic cancer. She had deteriorated suddenly and was in a lot of pain. They had hoped she would be able to die at home under the care of the hospice. In the final days Jack didn't think he could manage Peggy's care at home, and she was admitted to hospital where she later died.

When Jack came for help, his unhelpful thoughts (B) included the following:

I let Peggy down. I failed her. I feel so guilty that I couldn't care for her at home and let her die there in peace.

Using questions 1, 2 and 5, Jack began to challenge his thinking. He eventually was able to tell himself this.

There's no evidence that I failed Peggy. I tried my best but the disease got the better of us in the end. I wish things could have been different, but I know I did all I could. Peggy would say that going to hospital was the best decision given the circumstances and limited choices we had.

By thinking this way, Jack was able to change the way he thought and how he felt. Initially he felt guilt-stricken, which is considered a very destructive emotion. After he changed his thinking, his feelings of guilt dissipated. He still felt very sad and wished things had been different, but he wasn't blaming himself for doing something 'wrong'. Even though Jack rated the intensity of both his guilt and sadness at 8/10, by working through the framework he was able to let go of his guilt and stop blaming himself.

JACK'S DIARY ENTRY

A	B	C	D	E
Situation or trigger	Unhelpful thoughts	Feelings (score/10) Behaviour	Helpful thoughts	New feelings (score/10) New behaviour
Peggy died in hospital	*I failed Peggy*	Guilt (8/10)	*There's no evidence that I failed her; she would say that going to hospital was the best decision at the time.*	Sadness (8/10)

Whatever barriers you believe you are facing, take a moment to work through your thinking in the way Jack did – as outlined in exercise 4.5. Using the thought diary format, write down your answers in your journal.

EXERCISE 4.5: CHALLENGING YOUR UNHELPFUL THOUGHTS

Use the framework outlined in exercise 4.4 for any event or situation that is troubling you. You will find a blank thought diary form in Appendix 2, or you can use the thought diary format to write down your answers in your journal.

CONTINUE TO PRACTISE

Challenging your thoughts in this way takes practice, and it can feel difficult at first especially because of the content of your thoughts. Whenever you experience a strong negative reaction to a situation that has just happened, or to a memory of an event involving your loved one, stop what you are doing if you can and target your thinking. Ask yourself what you thought in the situation and identify those thoughts that are self-defeating and unhelpful. The key is to make sure that any new thoughts you generate are realistic and based on evidence. Challenging troubling thoughts in this way can be done in your scheduled 'grief time' as outlined in Chapter 3.

Guilt is an emotion people experience when they think they have done something wrong, whether or not they actually have. Any thoughts that lead to guilt need to be challenged.

Anger

With anger there will often be an identifiable cause – as with Paul whose son was killed by a drunk driver. The idea behind challenging your unhelpful thoughts is to try to shift the thinking patterns that are keeping you stuck and consumed by the anger, which in turn will change the way you feel. Over time Paul was able to change his unhelpful thinking. Initially he thought, *It's not fair, this guy who drinks and kills my son gets off without a scar.* When Paul was initially asked to rate the intensity of his anger on a scale of 0–10, he rated it as a 10.

Even though there is a real basis to Paul's anger, the problem was that it was consuming him and affecting his ability to move on with his life. It was taking up all his energy and preventing him from grieving the death of his son. When Paul challenged his thinking, he found question 3 (what is the likely effect on me of thinking this way?) particularly helpful in generating his new thoughts. In time he was able to say to himself, *It isn't fair that my son died, but focusing on the accident is keeping me from remembering my son. It is affecting my relationship with the rest of my family and also my work. I have to accept that bad things happen and I can't control that. This man has to live with the consequences of his actions for the rest of his life.* Eventually Paul rated his anger as 5/10. This reduction in the intensity of his anger meant that he was less consumed by it and more able to focus on his family and remember the happy times with his son.

PAUL'S DIARY ENTRY

A	B	C	D	E
Situation or trigger	**Unhelpful thoughts**	**Feelings (score/10)** **Behaviour**	**Helpful thoughts**	**New feelings (score/10)** **New behaviour**
Thinking about the drunk driver who killed my son	*This guy gets off without a scar*	Anger (10/10) Withdraws from family and friends	*It isn't fair, but focusing on the accident is affecting my life*	Anger (5/10) Tries to engage in normal routines

Challenging your thoughts in this way isn't a miracle cure. What you are attempting to do is to ensure that your thinking is helpful and accurate, which will allow you to grieve the loss of your loved one in a healthy way.

Sometimes people who have been bereaved express anger towards the medical staff who cared for their loved one. They may be angry that the correct diagnosis wasn't made earlier or that they couldn't cure their loved one. Often these feelings of anger can affect someone's ability to accept their loved one's death, as in Grahame's case.

> *She hadn't been feeling well for months and her doctor kept telling her she had a virus. It was too late by the time they finally found out that it was really her heart. She died a few days later. I am so angry. Why couldn't her doctor have done something sooner?*
>
> GRAHAME, 56

Grahame needed to challenge his thoughts otherwise he ran the risk of being consumed by his anger. By using the questions in exercise 4.4, Grahame eventually was able to tell himself, *Doctors aren't gods. I wish they could have diagnosed her condition sooner but it was a complicated case.* In time, by thinking this way, Grahame was able to accept the circumstances surrounding his wife's death even though he wished things could have been different.

Similarly Jessie struggled with feelings of anger towards her husband Bill's physician.

> *When Bill died I was very angry and upset with his doctor because he did not contact me after his death to offer his condolences. He had been Bill's doctor for twenty years and I thought he should have at least called or sent me a card to tell me how sorry he was. I can't stop thinking about this. I've decided to write him a letter to tell him how angry and disappointed I am in him.*
>
> JESSIE, 65

JESSIE'S DIARY ENTRY

A	B	C	D	E
Situation or trigger	**Unhelpful thoughts**	**Feelings (score/10)** **Behaviour**	**Helpful thoughts**	**New feelings (score/10)** **New behaviour**
Not hearing from the doctor after Bill died	*He should have contacted me*	Anger (8/10) Write a very angry letter	*I don't know why he didn't contact me.* *People don't always behave in the way you expect. Maybe there is a reason.*	Anger (5/10) Disappoint-ment (7/10) Write a composed letter

You can see from Jessie's diary entry that if she had written a letter based on her unhelpful thoughts, it would have probably been a very different one from the letter she did send after she challenged her thinking. She was able to reduce the intensity of her anger enough to write a composed letter outlining her disappointment.

SUGGESTION: WRITING LETTERS TO EXPRESS ANGER AND DISAPPOINTMENT

If you choose to write to someone to express your anger or hurt, don't send the letter or email for at least twenty-four hours after you have written it. Write it and save it. Often people write things in the heat of the moment only to regret their words later. Once twenty-four or even forty-eight hours have passed, reread what you have written and ask yourself the following questions. Is this really what I want to say? What are the likely consequences of sending this letter/email? Is there a better way to approach this? Waiting provides a buffer to protect you from saying words that you will not be able to retract at a later date, when you might think differently about the situation.

When my daughter was in her final days her husband would not allow me to visit her – he thought I would get too upset to see her the way she was. I am so angry and hurt by what he did that I'm not sure whether I can ever forgive him. I want to tell him how I feel but he seems to be avoiding me. I'm thinking about writing him a letter but I'd prefer to say what I need to say in person, so that I can hear what he has to say. My psychologist has suggested that I write down what I want to say to him, to organise my thoughts, and then arrange a time to meet him.

BETTY, 78

Regret

Regret is the emotion you experience when you wish things had turned out differently. Sometimes regret can turn into feelings of guilt if it's left unchecked. Consider Lara – she expressed regret about not saying 'I love you' to her mother before she died. Lara did not know her mother was going to die, so this is something she needed to remind herself of when she challenged her thinking about the last time she saw her mother.

LARA'S DIARY ENTRY

A	B	C	D	E
Situation or trigger	Unhelpful thoughts	Feelings (score/10) Behaviour	Helpful thoughts	New feelings (score/10) New behaviour
Thinking about mum's death	*Why didn't I tell her I loved her that last time?*	Regret (9/10) Sobbing	*I did not know she was going to die. I can't predict the future.*	Regret (5/10) Acceptance (5/10) Less crying

Being able to express all your thoughts and feelings, even if you are being hard on yourself, is a part of dealing with your grief. In the beginning you may just need to express your thoughts without challenging them. Sometimes just being able to express them brings clarity. Challenging unhelpful thoughts requires willingness and energy. It also takes practice.

Reconciling difficult relationships

Regret, guilt and anger often play a part in dealing with the death of a loved one if the relationship wasn't always easy. Maybe there were longstanding differences, misunderstandings or a distance that could not be bridged. Finding a way to reconcile the relationship and its difficulties is important in being able to accept your loved one's death and then move on. Exercise 4.6 can help you do this.

EXERCISE 4.6: RECONCILING DIFFICULT RELATIONSHIPS

This exercise will help you move on from your loved one's death. Use your journal to make notes as you work through this exercise.

Step 1. Identify the circumstances that were difficult in your relationship.

Step 2. In what way would you like them to have been different?

Step 3. What qualities did you appreciate about your loved one, despite your difficulties?

Step 4. What would you like to have said to your loved one about these difficulties?

Step 5. Write down these thoughts and read them aloud.

Step 6. What do you wish your loved one could have said to you? Write down these thoughts.

Step 7. Are you having unhelpful thoughts that are preventing you from being able to find a way to reconcile your relationship with your loved one? If you are, try challenging these thoughts using exercise 4.5.

I never felt that loved by my mother. She seemed to favour my brother and I always wondered whether I was good enough. I would have liked to have talked to her about this before she died but I never got a chance. It bothers me.

CAITLIN, 31

Unanswered questions

When there are unanswered questions surrounding the death of someone close to you, your brain is likely to go over and over all the possible explanations, often to the point of what seems like torture. Not knowing why or how someone died is a huge barrier to coming to terms with the death of a loved one. When something doesn't make sense your brain attempts to reconcile the facts as you know them. Often there are no answers. If you have unanswered questions you may feel better if you make an attempt to have your questions answered. This might mean speaking to the health professionals who were involved in your loved one's care, contacting the police who investigated their death, or researching a disease. In the case of suicide, trying to understand the events that led to the death could help. Did they leave a note for instance? Were they behaving erratically beforehand? Were they receiving counselling? Do other people have any information? You might also benefit from discussing your questions with a bereavement counsellor who can help you explore the possible answers. It's important to accept that you might never know or understand fully what happened. Similarly, your loved one's death could raise questions about your faith or spiritual life that you hadn't anticipated. If you have questions, arrange to speak to someone who can help you work through your concerns. Exercise 4.7 can help you identify the questions you want answered, whether or not you decide to seek professional help.

> *It's important to accept that you might never know or understand fully the circumstances surrounding your loved one's death.*

My dad died suddenly of an undiagnosed heart condition. We thought he had a virus so we all went into complete shock when we found out that he had died. There were so many questions that didn't have answers. Even his doctor seemed shocked. Nothing made sense and that first week was a total blur. What helped, though, was that we kept his appointment with the cardiologist who tried very hard to explain to us what he thought had happened. We recorded the session and then wrote out some of what he'd said and researched the medical condition. This all helped us a lot, but for the next year we still went over and over what we knew and what we didn't. It still doesn't make total sense but it certainly helped us to accept his death and move on with our lives.

ELLEN, 29

My daughter died at four months of age from Sudden Infant Death Syndrome (SIDS). She was a very happy baby and there were no signs that anything was wrong. Not knowing why she died or whether any other children we have might also have the same problem is consuming me.

TAYLOR, 32

EXERCISE 4.7: UNANSWERED QUESTIONS

Try working through these steps if you have questions about your loved one's death. Use your journal to make any notes.

Step 1. What questions do you have about the death of your loved one? Write them down.

Step 2. Is there any literature that might help you understand the situation more fully?

Step 3. Who could you contact to answer these questions?

Step 4. Set up an appointment with them, and explain why you are coming so they can prepare.

Step 5. Once you have this information, write down the possible answers to your questions – those that make the most sense to you.

After my husband died I worried that I hadn't done the right thing at the end. He was under hospice care – his pain seemed to be managed and he appeared to be comfortable. I had read the literature that our hospice nurse had given us about the signs of impending death and I thought I would know what to do. Just before he died he began to make a very disturbing gurgling noise. Even though I had read about the 'death rattle' I thought he was choking. I ended up calling the ambulance but he died before it arrived. This noise haunted me for several months after his death – I wondered whether he had actually choked to death. My bereavement counsellor arranged for me to talk to a hospice nurse who was able to explain the dying process more clearly and also the changes that occur when someone is actively dying. It helped a lot to hear her say that the events I relayed sounded very typical of the normal dying process, and that he hadn't choked to death.

ANNE, 58

Understanding suicide

If someone you loved died by suicide, you may be struggling with many unanswered questions or blaming yourself in some way. One of the most difficult aspects of suicide for those left behind is 'why?' Understanding the facts as you know them will help you reconcile – as best you can – why your loved one believed that suicide was their only choice. You might benefit from joining a support group for suicide survivors or from speaking to a mental health professional who can help you understand more fully the complexities of suicide. Your local or national suicide prevention organisation can suggest resources in your area. There is also a list of useful contacts in Appendix 3.

SUGGESTION: QUESTIONS ABOUT DEATH AND BEYOND

If the death of your loved one has raised questions or issues in relation to your faith or spirituality, you may benefit from speaking to someone about these concerns such as a minister, priest, rabbi or spiritual counsellor. Think about who you would feel most comfortable speaking to and arrange a time to meet them privately. Jot down your questions or concerns ahead of the meeting so you go prepared.

Why? It wasn't meant to be this way

If someone close to you has died prematurely, either suddenly or from an illness, you may well be struggling with the question 'why?' because the life you expected to unfold with your loved one is no longer a possibility. Trying to answer such questions is an important part of attempting to accept their death. Making some kind of sense of what has happened will take time, and may not be something that you can easily do on your own.

Typically the greater the discrepancy between how you expected your life to be and how it turned out, tends to predict how difficult it will be to reconcile or accept your loved one's death. In Stanley and Tina's cases, both found it very difficult to come to terms with the circumstances of their loss.

> *I worked hard all my life saving for our retirement. I wanted to earn as much money as I could so that when I died my wife would not have to worry about a thing. We always assumed I would be the first to die – I was ten years older and had more health issues. I never expected that she would die before me. My heart aches and I can't bear to be without her. I feel as though I am just waiting to die so that I can be with her again.*
>
> STANLEY, 71

Stanley benefited from being able to express his heartache over and over. He was eventually able to answer the 'why' when he accepted that neither he nor his wife could control the timing of their deaths, even though they had both assumed it would be the other way round.

> *I felt all the 'whys' were going to kill me after my baby son died from Sudden Infant Death Syndrome. Why did he die? Why didn't I go into his room earlier? Why us? I did everything you are told to do, so why did it happen? These questions rarely left me. You never expect things are going to happen to you, even though logically that doesn't make sense. But these things have to happen to someone. In the end the only way I could come to terms with his death, which brought me some peace, was to tell myself two things: that you can never know the real answer to 'why?'; and that I think he was only meant to touch our lives for a very short time.*

TINA, 29

Trying to make sense of what has happened will take time.

If you find that you are asking 'why?' about your loved one's death, try completing exercise 4.8.

EXERCISE 4.8: MAKING SENSE OF THE 'WHYS'

This exercise takes you through a series of questions that can help you begin to reconcile your 'whys'. Use your journal for any notes.

Step 1. What 'why?' questions do you have?

Step 2. What possible explanations can you list for each?

Step 3. If you have spiritual beliefs, which explanations fit the best?

Step 4. Are you having any thoughts that you need to challenge as you did in exercise 4.5?

Step 5. Now keeping in mind your beliefs about the world, write down the answers to your questions that make the most sense to you.

Step by step

When you start to take steps to tackle your worries – such as making a daily to do list and challenging the unhelpful thoughts that are keeping you stuck – you are, in fact, taking control of your grief rather than letting it control you. You are lessening the hold it has over you. There is no magic formula – what works for someone else may not work for you. Start with very small steps and keep your expectations realistic about what you can achieve. Keep in mind the wave-like nature of grief. In the next chapter we will focus specifically on your behaviour and the importance of choosing to act, even if you don't feel like it.

Summary

- Compartmentalise your worries
- Write a daily to do list
- Identify your barriers – what's keeping you stuck?
- Challenge unhelpful thoughts
- Attempt to answer questions you have surrounding the death of your loved one

5

Choose to act

The previous chapter introduced the importance of regaining a sense of control after someone dies. In particular you looked at your thoughts surrounding the death of your loved one, and how to go about challenging the ones that are self-defeating and keeping you stuck. The second important part of regaining control and moving forward with your life is turning your attention to your behaviour. This includes your daily routine, tackling difficult situations and speaking up about the help and support you need. This can be one of the hardest parts because it's contrary to what you feel like doing at the moment – nothing.

But I don't feel like doing anything

If your grief is new you might not feel like doing anything. You may just want to curl up in bed and not be disturbed. This is a very normal response. Or you might want to stay at home because you don't have the energy or motivation to go out and do the things you would usually do. You might fear bumping into someone you know and becoming overwhelmed with emotion, or you might be afraid to do things on your own that you once did with your loved one. Sometimes just going out and seeing other people happy in their lives is too much to bear as it's a stark reminder of how much you miss your loved one. It's hard not to notice all the other happy couples or families.

> *I can't leave my house since my husband died, other than to visit his grave. I just can't do it. I can't go to the shops because he always drove me. It all seems too much and I get very panicky – all I want to do is cry and stay at home. I don't want to see anyone.*
>
> MARGARET, 64

Sometimes you might need to 'do nothing'. But as a general rule of thumb, having things to do and commitments to keep will help you get through your day a little more easily. The aim is to take small steps – a day at a time or even just an hour at a time at the beginning. If you're distracted for a few moments each day by another person or task, or find something enjoyable for a minute or two, it helps in those early months. When you are feeling very sad or pining for your loved one, staying at home can actually make your grief harder to cope with: you have so much time on your hands to think about what has happened and to notice the absence of your loved one.

SUGGESTION: DISTRACTION IS GOOD FOR YOU

When your grief is new, getting through each hour is what you are trying to achieve. Finding things to distract you will give you a few moments of relief from your pain. Playing with children and pets, being with good friends, or seeing a movie can help – even if you don't think you'll be able to concentrate.

Doing something is usually better than doing nothing, even though you may find it extremely difficult. Rather than focusing on whether you feel like it or not, tell yourself that it is better for you to 'just do it'. If a friend or relative invites you to do something with them, say 'yes'. Don't wait to feel like doing it because it's unrealistic to think that you *will* feel like it for some time to come. Just give yourself a little nudge – most people say that they feel better for having done something. And establishing or re-establishing a routine is a good place to start.

Don't wait until you feel like doing something –
just do it!

My husband died in May after a short illness and I have found life without him unbearable. My doctor suggested I see a grief counsellor because I was having a very difficult time. She encouraged me to slowly get back into doing the things I used to enjoy, even if I didn't feel like it. I started walking again and going out with my friends. It was very hard – in the beginning I was really just going through the motions. But it did get easier and I did start to enjoy myself little by little.

TRISHA, 62

Establish a routine

If you are reading this book soon after your loved one has died, it's important to establish a daily routine no matter how simple. It might be getting out of bed each morning, having a shower and getting dressed. Or it may be driving to the shops to buy the morning newspaper. A routine helps so much because it eliminates the decision-making process. If you get up every day and have a particular cereal for breakfast, you don't have to decide what to eat each morning. When you are grieving, being able to do certain things automatically helps conserve your limited energy, especially in the early months. Use exercise 5.1 to help you establish your new routine.

EXERCISE 5.1 ESTABLISH YOUR ROUTINE

Again, use your journal to write down the details of your new routine. It's also a good idea to schedule time ahead for these regular activities in your diary or calendar.

Step 1. List the activities you used to do each day before the death of your loved one.

Step 2. Of these, which ones would be the easiest to resume?

Step 3. Use your calendar to plan what you will do, when and with whom. Start with the easiest activity and perhaps ask someone to go along with you the first time for support.

Step 4. Remember, don't wait until you feel like it – just do it.

Step 5. Add to your list each week.

Step 6. Incorporate the tasks from your daily to do list that you completed in Chapter 4, as well as things you used to find enjoyable, such as hobbies and exercise.

After my husband died I knew I had to do something — staying at home was driving me crazy. I was very active before he died: I used to swim regularly and the two of us bowled each week. I decided to go back to swimming first — it was easier because I had always done it on my own. Going back to bowls was harder and took me a little longer, but with the help of my friends I did it. I know that is what my husband would have wanted me to do.

FAITH, 66

EATING AND EXERCISING

It may sound clichéd, but eating well and being physically active are very important even when you're grieving. Aim to make both of them part of your daily routine. This not only helps to fill your day, but keeps you as healthy as possible when you are physically and emotionally vulnerable. Again you may say, *I don't feel like eating or exercising*. This may be true, but it comes back to not waiting until you *feel* like doing something. The trick is to just do it.

It is quite common to feel nauseous in the first few weeks, so start off with small and simple meals. Aim to eat at your regular meal times and try to eat something even if you have very little appetite — you'll need as much energy as possible. Many people report that they just don't have the motivation to prepare meals for one, especially if they used to cook for two. It's perfectly normal to feel like this, but if you find that not eating is becoming a problem for you, you'll need to work out what you can do differently.

When my husband died I decided it was pointless cooking meals just for one. I think my best meal in the first year after his death was an egg on toast.

DOROTHY, 65

SUGGESTION: THE MEANING OF FOOD

Meal times involve much more than just the consumption of food for energy. Meals are about social connections, interactions and family rituals. When someone you love dies, a chair at the table is empty and family rituals surrounding meals are altered. If eating is proving difficult for you, try to identify and challenge any unhelpful thoughts that could be keeping you stuck by using exercise 4.5.

We always used to talk about our day when we were preparing the evening meal. The house is so quiet now and I just eat a frozen dinner on my lap in front of the television.

PETER, 61

LOOKING AFTER YOURSELF: SOME TIPS ON HEALTHY EATING

- Plan to eat at regular meal times
- Try to eat what you normally would for breakfast, even if it's a smaller portion
- Eat meals that are easy to prepare
- Prepare a double quantity and freeze the other portion
- Invite someone over for dinner
- Limit highly processed and 'fast' foods
- Limit your alcohol intake
- Eat lots of fruit and vegetables
- Challenge your thinking about food preparation and eating if it's unhelpful

Some people turn to food for comfort – 'comfort food' – and gain weight following the death of their loved one, which unfortunately only makes them feel worse. If you are prone to putting on weight, try to follow the tips on healthy eating and build your meals into your daily routine. At the end of this chapter you will find other constructive things to do to help bring you comfort as you grieve.

SUGGESTION: A NOTE ABOUT ALCOHOL

Alcohol is a depressant and it can interfere with your sleep. If you find you are using alcohol to numb your pain you should avoid drinking it.

These same principles also apply to exercise – start off by doing just a little bit each day and build it into your daily routine. Remember to be realistic in what you choose to do and find something that you enjoy. A short walk to get out of the house is a great place to start. Depending on what exercise you usually do, start with whatever's easiest and build up gradually. People often report that they find walking, swimming and yoga very therapeutic, especially as they can do them at their own pace. Team sports can also be rewarding, but they might be harder to do at first because they involve commitment and a lot of social interaction, which you might not yet be quite up to.

LOOKING AFTER YOURSELF: SOME TIPS ON EXERCISING

- Doing something is better than doing nothing
- Walk wherever you can
- Take the stairs

- Walk a dog (even if it's not your own)
- Be realistic about what you can achieve
- Try to build some form of activity into your daily routine
- Build up gradually

I always loved to walk as I enjoyed being outside, alone with my thoughts. When my son was killed I knew walking would be good for me, but I didn't want to be alone with my thoughts because they were too painful. So I listened to music while I walked.

KIM, 44

SLEEP DISTURBANCE

Many people who are grieving say that they just can't sleep. It's always a good idea to check in with your doctor if you've had trouble sleeping for more than a few weeks. Even though sleeping tablets are not recommended for long-term use, your doctor might want to prescribe them for a short period of time.

Try these strategies first if you're having difficulty falling asleep. Follow your usual sleeping patterns and anchor your bedtime each night, so you get into a routine. It's also a good idea to aim to get up at the same time each day so that sleeping in doesn't affect falling asleep at night. If your thoughts are racing, add them to your 'worry boxes' or your to do list to help shut them off (see exercises 4.1 and 4.2). Exercising in the morning or early afternoon may help tire you out before bed. You might also find that a warm bath or listening to soothing music just before bed can help. But limit your caffeine and alcohol intake. Above all try not to panic if you can't sleep because this will only make matters worse.

Often people say that they don't have trouble falling asleep but that they wake up early and can't get back to sleep. Here are a few suggestions if you find that you can't fall back to sleep.

LOOKING AFTER YOURSELF: SOME TIPS ON GETTING BACK TO SLEEP

- Read for a while and see if you feel sleepy again
- Have a drink of warm milk
- Keep a notepad by your bed so you can write down anything that's worrying you. Tell yourself that you will think about these issues in the morning, and add them to your 'worry boxes' or to do list
- Tell yourself that sleep disturbance is a normal reaction following the death of a loved one and is usually only temporary
- If nothing works, get up and start your day

For more information on tackling sleep problems, read *Overcoming Insomnia and Sleep Problems* by Colin Espie – another book in the *Overcoming* series.

Sleep disturbance is a normal reaction to the death of a loved one. Consult your doctor if you are having prolonged difficulty sleeping.

Framework for making difficult decisions

The list of issues that need to be resolved in some way after a loved one's death can seem endless. Using a framework to make any decision you are facing – not just about issues concerning your grief – can make the process much easier. Exercise 5.2 outlines a standard framework that encourages realistic thinking about difficult decisions by focusing on the possible consequences of certain outcomes. If you use this framework to make decisions, you are far less likely to make an impulsive decision that you may regret in the future.

EXERCISE 5.2: FRAMEWORK FOR MAKING DIFFICULT DECISIONS

Use your journal to note down your answers as you work through this exercise. Alternatively, you will also find a blank framework form in Appendix 2.

Step 1. What is the problem you are experiencing or the decision you are facing?

Step 2. How many possible solutions can you list?

Step 3. What are the positives and negatives of each of these possible solutions?

Step 4. Which looks best to you?

Step 5. If you used this solution, what would the consequences be?

Step 6. Can you live with these consequences? Yes/No

Step 7. If you answered 'no' in step 6, go back to step 2 and work through the remaining steps again.

Step 8. If you use the solution you identified in step 4, what action do you need to take to try out this solution?

You can use this framework to make decisions about your life now or to make decisions with other family members about matters relating to your loved one's estate, such as finalising affairs and distributing personal belongings.

Let's look at an example. When Jane, Susan and Bob's father died, the family home was left to them equally as their mother had died several years earlier. Each child had a different idea about what to do with the home. The children all got on very well but were afraid of hurting each other's feelings. They decided to use the framework for making difficult decisions to help them work out what to do. The three of them met one afternoon to consider their options. By working through their decision in this way, they were able really to think through the issues and make the best decision possible – even though that meant the outcome might not be what they had wanted individually. Working methodically through difficult decisions using this framework minimises the chance that you will make a decision based on emotion that you might regret in the future. Plus it is a vehicle for opening up discussions with others.

FRAMEWORK FOR MAKING DIFFICULT DECISIONS: JANE, SUSAN AND BOB'S ANSWERS

Step 1.   What is the problem you are experiencing or the decision you are facing?

Working out what to do with the family home.

Step 2.   How many possible solutions can you list?

Jane: wants to sell it and divide the money equally.

Susan: wants to rent it and divide the income equally.

Bob: wants to buy out his sisters, renovate and live there himself.

Step 3.   What are the positives and negatives of each of these possible solutions?

Jane's option: + simple, fair; – house no longer in family.

Susan's option: + house remains in family; – upkeep, dealing with tenants, complicated.

Bob's option: + house remains in family, will enjoy renovating it; – can't really afford to keep it, renovating is lots of work, likes where living now, sense of unfairness for sisters.

Step 4.   Which looks best to you?

   Jane's option.

Step 5.   If you used this solution, what would the consequences be?

   The house would no longer be in the family.

Step 6.   Can you live with these consequences? Yes/No

   Yes.

Step 7.   If you answered 'no' in step 6, then go back to step 2 and work through the remaining steps again.

Step 8.   If you used the solution you identified in step 4, what action do you need to take to try out this solution?

   1.   *Give everyone a cooling-off period of two weeks to really think about this option.*

   2.   *If everyone agrees, then contact estate agents to have the property valued.*

   3.   *If someone changes their mind within this period, begin again at step 2.*

Returning to work – when is the best time?

This is a question many people ask. The answer to this is that it depends. You might not have the luxury of choosing when to return to work due to your company's bereavement policy, or the fact that you've got bills to pay. From a healthy grieving perspective, a general guideline is to return to work as soon as you think you can, rather than when you *feel* like it. Most people say that they feel better when they're at work because they are occupied with something else other than their loss, and benefit from the social support and interaction with their colleagues.

> *Going back to work was the best thing I did – it distracted me from my own thoughts. It helped a lot too that my colleagues were very supportive and I knew the routine. Coming home to an empty house was the hardest thing.*
>
> GRACE, 59

Some people return to work on reduced hours and gradually build back up to their normal duties. There will of course be exceptions to this rule. Gina and David's situations are two such examples.

> *Before my husband became ill I had been thinking about changing jobs – I didn't like the company I was with or the job itself. After he died I took a leave of absence and to this day, six months later, I haven't returned. I need the money but I just don't think I can go back because*

the job is too stressful. I've decided to see if I can find something else.

GINA, 51

When my wife died I took an extended leave of absence from work because I had our children to care for. They were really young at the time and losing their mother was very tough. I felt I needed to be at home taking care of everything she normally did, to make it easier on them. Slowly I'm working out how best to return to work because I will need to do that at some stage. Luckily I'm in the position to be able to take the time I need.

DAVID, 43

SUGGESTION: CONTACT HUMAN RESOURCES

If you are reading this book soon after the death of your loved one, contact your Human Resources department at work or ask someone to do it on your behalf. Find out what leave is available to you – there could be options you haven't considered.

I took a week off work after my mother died. My boss was great and said I could have more time if I needed it, but being at home thinking about everything was driving

*me crazy. I went back to work and my colleagues were so
supportive. They gave me my space but were also there if
I needed to talk. Going back to work really helped me.
The weekdays were much better than the weekends.*

NATASHA, 29

Targeting what you've lost

You lose many things when someone dies, apart from the person. In Chapter 3, exercise 3.1 helped you identify all the roles your loved one assumed. Part of grieving is working through these separate losses and finding ways to either come to terms with them or work out how best to replace what's missing. Some things of course cannot be replaced; other losses may be replaced in a different way.

I hate Sundays

It's not surprising that some people who have recently been bereaved hate Sundays or the weekends. Many say that Sundays – or perhaps other days, depending on your culture – are their worst day. It's a time when families are together and the pace of life is a little slower, which means you have more time to think about what has happened. If a specific day of the week is difficult for you, then make a plan for that day each week. Remember, though, that you can't rely on someone else calling you to arrange your day. It's up to you. Knowing that the day is coming gives you time to prepare – exercise 5.3 will help you make a plan.

EXERCISE 5.3: PREPARING FOR A SPECIFIC DAY

Step 1. Which day of the week are you dreading? List the activities you used to do on that day.

Step 2. Add any other activities you can think of that are possible for you to do now on that day.

Step 3. Rank them in order of enjoyment from the least enjoyable to most enjoyable.

Step 4. Starting at the top of your list with the most enjoyable activity, circle the ones that would be easiest for you to do now.

Step 5. Select one activity from your list that you would like to try next time this day comes around.

Step 6. Keep this list handy so you can refer to it when you need an idea about what to do.

My wife and I did everything together after I retired. Sundays were a day when we went out or the kids and grandchildren came to visit. I dread Sundays now that

she is gone because I don't know what to do with myself.
The kids ask me over but I don't want to go every week
— I feel as if I'm imposing even though they tell me I'm
not. So what I decided to do was to get a part-time job
on a Sunday. That has really helped me get through my
Sundays.

TIM, 62

Dealing with loneliness

Feelings of loneliness may be a particularly common problem if someone close to you has died. Even if you are surrounded by your friends and family, you might still feel 'alone' and long to be with your loved one. This is perfectly normal. Part of coming to terms with their death is adjusting to all the different changes in your life at a physical, emotional and cognitive level.

Targeting both your thoughts and your behaviour is the best approach to dealing with loneliness. In much the same way as you did in Chapter 4, you need to make sure your thinking is helpful and realistic, such as in the following examples.

- It is normal to feel lonely or alone following the death of a loved one
- In time, as I adjust to life without them, my feelings of loneliness will diminish

---

- I need to target my loneliness by planning to do things with other people even though I will still feel lonely
- I need to be patient with myself
- Yearning or pining for my loved one is normal and it will lessen in time

Tackling avoidance

If you've been avoiding a certain place or person since your loved one died, you need to decide how to tackle your avoidance because it will only make things harder in the long run. Many people avoid certain rooms in their house, favourite restaurants, visiting their loved one's grave or talking to others about the death. You may fear losing control of your emotions and avoid putting yourself in certain situations. But there is a fine line between not being ready to face something and avoiding it. It's likely that you'll know which category you fall into. Unfortunately the problem with avoidance is that while it may help ease your pain in the beginning, it will only make your grief worse in the long term.

After my husband died I found it very difficult to spend time in our living room. Everything in there reminded me of him, especially 'his' chair. My grief counsellor suggested that I gradually spend more time each evening in the living room, which I did. Eventually it got much easier and now it brings me some kind of peace because I feel close to him – especially when I sit in 'his' chair.

ROSE, 67

The framework outlined in exercise 5.4 will help you tackle any situation that you are avoiding.

EXERCISE 5.4: FRAMEWORK FOR TACKLING AVOIDANCE

Step 1. What places are you avoiding?

Step 2. What people are you avoiding?

Step 3. What activities are you avoiding?

Step 4. For each item you listed above, what do you fear would happen if you didn't avoid them?

Step 5. Rank the items you listed in steps 1–3, starting with the easiest to confront.

Step 6. For each one, write down what you think about the item you are avoiding.

Step 7. As you did in Chapter 4, challenge any unhelpful or self-defeating thoughts using the five questions from exercise 4.4 (below). Write down your new, helpful thoughts.

1. Where's the evidence for what I thought?

2. What are the alternatives to what I thought?

3. What is the likely effect on me of thinking in this way?

4. How would I advise a friend to think in the same situation?

5. What would my loved one tell me if they were here now?

Step 8. Plan how you can gradually approach the items you are avoiding, beginning with the least difficult. If possible break down each item into smaller steps, beginning with the least difficult step.

Let's consider two different examples, Roslyn and Michael.

My husband and I went out regularly with five other couples who we have known since our children were babies. We would go out as a large group once every few weeks. After my husband died our friends were all very supportive and wanted me to continue going out as we always did. At first I just couldn't go, even though I knew it would be best for me. I felt like a fish out of water and the more they insisted, the more anxious I became. The grief counsellor I saw helped me work out a plan. Gradually I did things with the group. At first I invited just the women over to my house. Then the men as well. Eventually I could go out with everyone. It's much easier now and I'm so glad I persisted, otherwise I would have lost a great source of support.

ROSLYN, 60

For Roslyn, resuming social contact with a group of friends who had been a significant part of her life with her husband was going to be very emotionally charged. Tackling this situation using a gradual approach increased her sense of control, and allowed her to better manage the anxiety she was experiencing.

After my brother Josh died by suicide, I refused to drive past his house for months even though it was on my way home. Somehow I figured that if I didn't go that way I could convince myself that he was still alive. One day I was with a friend who happened to drive that way and I totally lost it.

MICHAEL, 22

Let's look at how Michael answered the questions using the framework for tackling avoidance.

FRAMEWORK FOR TACKLING AVOIDANCE,
MICHAEL'S ANSWERS

Step 1.   What places are you avoiding?

My brother's house.

Step 4.   For each item you listed above, what
do you fear would happen if you didn't
avoid them?

*I fear that I will break down, get angry and
smash something.*

Step 6.   For each item, write down what you
think about the item you are avoiding.

*I think that if I don't drive past his house I can
pretend he didn't kill himself.*

Step 7.   As you did in Chapter 4, challenge any
unhelpful or self-defeating thoughts using
the five questions from exercise 4.4.
Write down your new helpful thoughts.

*I know Josh did die. I'm not sure of all the rea-
sons why he did it, but he was pretty depressed
at the time. By avoiding his street I am only*

---

making it worse as I'm always thinking about how not to drive that way. It's okay for me to be upset and angry and I do need to express these feelings – just not in a destructive way.

Step 8. Plan how you can gradually approach the item you are avoiding, beginning with the least difficult. If possible break down each item into smaller steps, beginning with the least difficult step.

I am going to drive past his house with my friend first. If I get upset, that is okay. I will ask my friend to stay with me and plan what to do afterwards. I will do it each day until I can do it on my own.

Michael was able to begin to take control of his life again by tackling his avoidance in this way. Until this point the avoidance behaviour was holding him hostage. Even though it was very hard to drive past his brother's home, Michael broke down what seemed like an enormous and painful task into smaller, more manageable steps. Asking for help from his friend provided a buffer until he was ready to face it on his own.

EXERCISE 5.5: WHAT ARE YOU AVOIDING?

Are you avoiding someone or something to do with the death of your loved one? Use the framework for tackling avoidance (exercise 5.4) to plan how you can approach what you are avoiding in a gradual way. You will find a blank framework form in Appendix 2.

My sister died many years ago when we were teenagers. Now as a grown woman with children of my own, her death still haunts me. She died tragically and somehow I blame myself for what happened, even though I know it isn't true. I won't go to her grave and I am very protective and strict with my children about what they can and can't do. They are starting to resent me and I know I have to do something about it because I'm pushing them away. I know I need to go to the grave. And I know I need to talk to someone about her death.

CARMEN, 45

If you are having difficulty facing something and don't believe you can tackle it on your own, you might benefit from consulting a grief counsellor or a clinical psychologist. They will be able to help you examine your thinking and face the situations you are avoiding in a gradual way.

Avoiding difficult situations only makes grief worse.
Seek help if you can't confront them on your own.

Your tool box

One common theme throughout *Overcoming Grief* is that 'it's up to you' to find the support you need during this difficult time. People often feel let down by their friends and family because they haven't called when they said they would, or they've made hurtful remarks about 'getting on with life'. Grief is hard enough as it is, without extra hurt or anger added into the mix. Unless someone has experienced something very similar – and even then there are no guarantees because grief is unique – it is really up to you to explain what you need at this time. Hoping or expecting that those closest to you will know how to help you is setting yourself up for more heartache.

The concept of a tool box is a useful framework for understanding what you need to do to help yourself when you are grieving. In your tool box, there will be different types of tools or strategies to help you cope with your loss. There might be tools to help you express your thoughts and feelings to others, there might be tools to help you develop new routines or to acknowledge difficult days, and so on. And because everyone grieves in their own way, the contents of your tool box will be different to someone else's. We've now covered a number of different strategies that you could use in your tool box to help you adjust to life without your loved one. These include keeping a grief journal, working through difficult feelings, exercising, attending a support group or seeing a counsellor. Using the tool box concept as a framework, think about what types of things will help ease your pain. What has helped so far?

Only you can decide what is best for you and what will bring you comfort. Working out what tools you need in your tool box is the next step, and exercise 5.6 will help you do this.

EXERCISE 5.6: WHAT DO YOU NEED IN YOUR TOOL BOX?

Tick off the items you think would be helpful in supporting you through your grief. List any others you think of in the space provided.

Music
Yoga
Massage
Exercise
Seeing a bereavement counsellor
Attending a bereavement support group
Talking to a friend who can listen to my pain
Writing regularly in a journal about my grief
Making a memory book (see Chapter 7)
Writing my loved one's story (see Chapter 7)
Being with family
Being with friends

Being alone
Returning to work
Volunteering
Trying something new
Having a holiday
Reading self-help books
Getting a pet
Joining an online support group
Being assertive – saying 'no' to requests
Advocating for what I need
Seeing a clinical psychologist
Maintaining realistic expectations of my progress

_____

_____

_____

_____

_____

Once you've ticked off the items you think will benefit you, it's time to take action. In much the same way as you did in Chapter 4 where you generated a daily to do list, choose which of the ticked items on the list you'd like to do first. Some will take more planning, such as going on a holiday, so start by selecting the items that are easiest to put into practice. For example you might have ticked off attending a bereavement support group, reading self-help books and writing in a journal. You could buy a journal and some self-help books on the same day. Finding a support group will take more time. You might need to look online or contact your local hospice or community health service to see what groups are available in your area. Be prepared to try different things. You can always add to your list.

When should you seek help?

Too often people believe that they should be able to solve their own problems without the help of others. Unfortunately this mindset perpetuates the myth that seeking help is a sign of weakness. In fact coming to terms with the death of a loved one is a huge task and not one to be done without support. For some people, dealing with their pain may be so overwhelming that they try to disconnect from their feelings. This might help in the beginning, but unfortunately it can also make matters worse.

The following signs may be an indication that you would benefit from speaking to a health professional who specialises in working with people who have been bereaved.

- Feeling depressed
- Feeling hopeless about your future
- Thinking about suicide or not being here anymore
- Feeling as though you are getting worse
- Being consumed by the death of your loved one
- Avoiding thinking about your loved one
- Avoiding talking about your loved one or anything that reminds you of them
- Withdrawing from others
- Relying heavily on alcohol or other drugs
- Having difficulty attending work, university or school
- Experiencing marked disturbances in your sleep and appetite

Even if your loved one died some years ago it's never too late to seek help, especially if you believe that their death is affecting your life now. Laura's story is a good example. It highlights that grief can fester like an untreated wound if it is not expressed.

I had just become engaged and the first person I called was my mum! Had I not been drinking champagne I would have driven the five hours from London to my parents' home immediately. I went the following weekend instead – it was 19 January 1991 and I was brimming with excitement and ideas for reception venues. When I arrived at my childhood home, my father was slouched at the kitchen table. He looked up and said, 'Your mum has had a stroke, she's in a coma and I don't think she'll last the night.' The shock was immeasurable; she was seemingly fit and healthy. We drove to the hospital. My mum never regained consciousness and I was with her when she died a few hours later. On the day of her funeral Cornwall suffered the worst gales in fifty years. I don't think she was ready to leave us either.

I didn't want to wake up in the morning and feel the awful sinking feeling in my stomach when I realised it wasn't a dream. I just wanted things to go back to how they were. I didn't want to think about what my life was going to be like without her. Over the next few months my emotions ranged from complete refusal to believe what had happened, immense loss, anger and grief, to a feeling of wanting to push and break all the boundaries that until then I had been quite happy to accept. I felt as though nothing mattered anymore.

Everyone grieves in their own way and I am very private. I don't let people in; I push them away. I felt as though I was being sucked into a downward spiral. I'd become 'unengaged', cancelling the wedding and leaving my partner feeling helpless, not knowing what to do. I knew I had to do something to get my life back on track and that I couldn't do it alone. I went to see someone but these visits didn't help at all. The counsellor implied that my mum's influence over me was in part responsible for the angst I was feeling. I found it hard to share my precious thoughts and memories about the person who had meant the most to me in my life, with someone who didn't even know her or me. I resented her comments and stopped going after two visits.

My relationship miraculously stood the test of time. Rather than dealing with my grief I think I just pushed it down into a big pit. I was no longer the fun-loving bouncy person of my youth. I married my partner and had three children. I didn't allow myself to feel the loss of not being able to share those special occasions with my mother. I felt as though I could no longer experience real happiness. My grief had put a ceiling over my emotions – maybe it was self-protection. My last experience with happiness went hand in hand with the saddest moment in my life, and I didn't ever want to go through anything like that again.

Many years later a very dear friend suggested I try talking to a clinical psychologist who specialised in grief. I took her advice and making my first appointment was the first step in my healing process. People say that time is a great healer, but I think the extent to which you heal is governed by your ability to confront and deal with your grief and accept what has happened. Over the years I had pushed my grief away, not wanting to deal with it. It was only after my therapy that this became clear to me. It was a very hard process. I don't like crying in front of people and I would try to suppress my sobbing, but I couldn't talk about my memories or feelings without the floodgates opening.

One of the hardest things for me was that I never got the chance to tell my mother all the things I would have liked to say, like how much I loved her and how much she meant to me. My therapist suggested I write down all those thoughts in a letter. I thought that was hard enough, but the hardest part was reading my letter to mum aloud. I was given the option not to, but I knew I had to be able to move on. That was the final release for me – I let out all the emotion that I'd kept pushed inside for so long. I accepted my mum's death and I chose to move on with my life.

LAURA, 45

Continue to take action

We have covered a lot of ground in this chapter and you might need to go over it from time to time as you move forward. Being mindful of what you say to yourself about your situation, and of what you do, are two major factors that you need to address continually. As hard as it is to hear, overcoming grief is a solitary pursuit because no one can do it for you. But it is not something that you have to do without support. There will be many hurdles for you to overcome, including difficult questions that you might have and tricky conversations with those around you. The next chapter will outline a number of strategies or tools that will help you tackle difficult conversations with children, family members, friends and colleagues.

Summary

- Don't wait until you feel like doing something – just do it
- Establish a daily routine
- Gradually face difficult situations
- It's up to you to get the support you need
- Continue to add to your tool box

6

Difficult conversations

You will have to have many difficult conversations after someone dies. Conversations with children, family members, friends and work colleagues. These will be about the death itself, and in the months following about how you are 'coping' and what well-meaning friends or family think you should be doing. Some of these conversations will be more difficult than others, especially those that happen when you least expect them. But they might be a little easier if you can think about what you might say ahead of time. When you are grieving, saying what you think is far better than hoping that others will know what you want. Unfortunately lots of people don't 'do' grief well, so taking the lead by speaking up for yourself about what you need is another important aspect of taking control of your grief. This chapter focuses on conversations with children about the death of their loved one, as well as conversations you might have with other adults.

Talking with children

Like adults, children grieve. What is different is the way they express their grief, which will be largely dependent on two things.

- The nature of the relationship the child had with the person who died
- The child's age and developmental level

Children will grieve in their own way and individual differences play a large role. Some will be able to express their thoughts and feelings verbally whereas others may do this through their behaviour. They might regress and you could see behaviours that you thought they had outgrown such as bed-wetting or thumb-sucking. They might become very clingy and not let you out of their sight. Young children will often play games about death and dying which can cause adults concern. These games are perfectly normal and healthy because they allow children to express their feelings and perhaps make sense of something that they can't readily verbalise. Table 6.1 outlines what you might expect at certain ages based on a child's understanding of death.

When my wife died from ovarian cancer, my son was nine and my daughter seven. We had used a hospice and the children knew that their mother was very sick. What amazed me was how differently they both expressed their grief in the months that followed. My son was very quiet and seemed withdrawn, whereas my daughter was very verbal – always talking about her mother and asking lots of questions. They both tested the limits at times and seemed to need lots of attention from me. I realised that the way in which they were showing their feelings was in keeping with their personalities: my son is usually the quiet one and my daughter the talker. I just make sure that I give both of them lots of opportunities to talk with me about their mum.

SAM, 44

TABLE 6.1 CHILDREN'S UNDERSTANDING OF DEATH AT DIFFERENT AGES

UNDER 3S

- Cognitively unable to understand the concept of death
- Will sense the reactions of those around them
- Might show distress as a result of separation from the person who has died

AGES 3–5

- Death is seen as temporary and reversible
- Very concrete thinkers
- May ask the same questions over and over again to make sure nothing has changed
- Can be clingy, regress in their behaviour, demonstrate separation anxiety and experience sleeping difficulties

- Tend to express their thoughts and feelings through their play

AGES 6-8

- Understand that death is irreversible
- Think you can 'escape' it
- Don't believe that it could happen to them
- Might show aggressive behaviour, have difficulty sleeping and fear being alone

AGES 9-11

- Death is understood as final and irreversible
- Great interest in the scientific and biological aspects of death
- Might appear cold

AGES 12 +

- Have an adult understanding of death
- Death shatters their view of immortality
- Might engage in risk-taking behaviours in an attempt to test the limits of their immortality
- Can be very emotional
- Might not share their thoughts or feelings with other family members
- Prefer to be with their peer group

Taking the lead

Even though children may often be kept in the background when someone dies, they will be affected by how others respond to the news of the death. They are perceptive and can readily pick up cues from those around them. Often children react more to how others are behaving and to what is or isn't being said, than to the news of the death itself. It can be very confusing and distressing for children to see their own parents or other family members distraught, especially if the death was sudden and unexpected. Letting children know why those around them are behaving the way they are will help them understand some of what is going on. It's best to be up front with children as they usually can sense when things aren't right, and hiding the truth will only make matters worse. They might also worry about their own future and the implications of the death on their life. Again, take the lead in discussions and be open with the facts as you know them.

Explain to children the truth about the cause of death, using language that is simple and appropriate for their age and developmental level.

Children also tend to be very egocentric, believing that the world revolves around them. Because of this, some children might wonder whether they did something to cause the death of their loved one, even though they might not verbalise this fear. This is why it is important to explain the truth about the cause of the death to children of all ages. It's also important to use language that is appropriate for their age and development – in much the same way as you would tailor any conversation about sexual reproduction.

Breaking the news

The best approach to telling a child that a loved one has died is to tell them honestly, using the word 'died'. Use terms that are accurate and avoid euphemisms, which can easily confuse children. Even though adults often use the phrase 'passed away' or 'passed on', these are unfamiliar words to a child and can lead to confusion. Similarly, telling a child that death is like sleep can create great anxiety about sleeping. Even though you may be very upset, don't shy away from letting children see your emotion – they need to learn that it is normal to be sad and to cry when somebody you love dies.

Don't use euphemisms such as 'passed away', 'passed on' or 'gone to sleep'. Children find these phrases very confusing.

This is a conversation a mother had with her 10-year-old daughter, to tell her that her grandmother had died.

Mother: Katie, Mummy wants to tell you some sad news.

Grandma died today at about 11 this morning. As you know she had been sick for a long time and was in the nursing home.

Katie: What did she die from?

Mother: Well, the doctors said that she died from an illness called pneumonia and because she was very old her body couldn't fight the pneumonia and her heart and lungs just stopped working.

Katie: Does that happen to people your age too?

Mother: Usually if people my age get the same illness, they would be much stronger and wouldn't die. I am fit and healthy and a lot younger than Grandma.

In this part of the conversation you can see that Katie is initially concerned that her mother could also die. Katie's mum was able to answer her question simply and honestly, providing her with the reassurance she needed. It's also important to realise that Katie's grief will be different to her mother's. Even though Katie might have been very close to her grandmother, her own mother is her focus. A child may become more upset by seeing their parent distressed than from the actual loss of their grandparent. This is totally normal and expected, especially as the relationship and connection they had with their grandparent will, in most cases, be different to the relationship and connection an adult child had with their own parent.

Katie's focus turned to her own death as the conversation continued.

Katie: Mummy, why are you crying so much?

Mother: I'm just very sad that Grandma died. I will be okay, Katie - I just miss her. When people die who we love it's okay to cry and be sad.

Katie: Would you cry, Mummy, if I died?

Mother: Of course, darling. I'd cry for a very, very long time.

Katie: How old do you think I will be when I die?

Mother: No one knows the answer to that question but we all die at some stage. Most people live to be quite old. Now let's start getting some favourite photos of Grandma to make a collage for her funeral.

Again you can see the mother has answered Katie's questions honestly. Katie is viewing this experience through her world, which is very normal for a 10-year-old. The mother is using each opportunity to role-model a healthy grief response for her daughter. When Katie asked about the age she would be when she dies, her mother was honest, telling her no one knows the answer to that question. Her answers are factual, while at the same time reassuring. She then diverts Katie away from her own thoughts of death back to her Grandmother's death, where she invites Katie to help her look for photos for the funeral.

Use the guidelines below if you need to talk to a child about the death of a loved one.

GUIDELINES FOR TALKING TO CHILDREN ABOUT DEATH

- Tell children the truth about the death in simple terms
- Use language appropriate for their age and developmental level. Use the word 'died'
- Encourage them to ask questions
- Answer their questions honestly and simply
- Avoid euphemisms and convoluted responses that can cause confusion
- Explain the physical facts of death using accurate terms
- If you do not know the answer to a question, say so
- Be prepared to answer the same question over and over again
- Tell them it's okay to be sad and to cry
- Let them know that adults are sad too
- Let them know that the death wasn't their fault
- Keep children with the family as much as possible
- Include children in the funeral arrangements if appropriate
- Encourage them to say goodbye to their loved one, which might involve viewing the body
- Encourage them to write a poem or letter, or make a card, to be placed in the coffin with their loved one
- Keep children informed about what is happening at all times

Framework for informing children about a death

The following framework will help you prepare for breaking the news to children if you are anticipating the death of a loved one, even though you can never predict exactly how events will unfold. Consider the four 'Ws' in exercise 6.1: who, what, when and where.

EXERCISE 6.1 FRAMEWORK FOR INFORMING CHILDREN ABOUT A DEATH

Consider these questions carefully and write down your thoughts in your journal.

Step 1. Who is the best person to tell the child about the death?

Step 2. What information should the child be told about the circumstances of the death?

Step 3. When should the child be told?

Step 4. Where should the child be told and who else should be there?

When my husband was dying of cancer our hospice team helped me to work out, as well as I could, how I would tell our 12- and 10-year-olds of their dad's death when the time came. The kids knew that their father was dying and had been involved all along. The nurses told me when they thought it was close, but we tried to keep things as normal as possible. My husband died when the kids were at school, which gave me some time on my own with him. I told them when they got home and took them together into the room to say their last goodbyes. It was very tough but I needed to be the one to do it.

JANETTE, 46

How you answer the questions in exercise 6.1 will depend on: who died and how close the children were to the person who died; whether or not the death was expected; what time of day or night the death occurred; and how their parent(s) or caregiver(s) has been affected by the news of the death. Let's look at each question in a little more detail.

WHO?

Usually the best person to break the news is the person closest to the child who is *emotionally* capable of doing so. If the child's parent(s) or caregiver(s) is deeply affected by the news of the death – as in the case of the death of their spouse/partner, the child's other parent, or the child's brother or sister – it might be necessary to ask someone else to oversee the child's well-being for a short period of time. This person could be a favourite aunt or uncle, an older cousin, a step-parent or a trusted family friend. The important thing is for the child to be with someone they are close to.

WHAT?

What information a child is told needs to be agreed between the parents or caregivers. Each child needs to be told the same story. They will probably ask many questions and you need to be consistent in your approach. If the circumstances surrounding the death are tragic, you will need to decide beforehand exactly how much information you will tell the child. Telling the truth is considered to be the best approach, otherwise you risk children finding out from other sources. Even though such conversations may be difficult, start with the basic facts and let the child ask questions. Be prepared for the child to ask more questions as they begin to comprehend what has happened.

WHEN?

As a general rule tell the child about the death as soon as possible to minimise the chance that someone else will tell them first, and before they gather something is wrong from what is happening around them. If they are at school you will need to decide whether to pick them up early or wait until they get home. Having some extra time while they are at school might give you the opportunity to decide what you need to do next.

WHERE?

Where the child is told will depend on the circumstances

and who will be telling them. Depending on the child's age and personality, you might want to arrange for a friend or family member to be with them for a while after they have been told. Some children will not want to leave your side, especially if they are worried about you.

> *My husband was killed in a car accident. The police officer came to my house at about one o'clock in the morning to tell me he had died. My kids were sleeping at the time but luckily my sister was visiting me that week. We decided not to wake the children and told them in the morning, together. I was in shock and just having those few hours helped me work out what I was going to say to them.*
>
> CAROLINE, 33

Unexpected and tragic death

Unfortunately, in the case of a sudden and unexpected death of a close relative, there is no easy way to tell a child other than to do it simply, honestly and with great compassion. A child's comprehension of death will very much depend on their age and whether or not they have experienced other deaths. For many children the death of a pet will be their first significant loss. Helping children understand that death is a normal part of life can help them grasp more fully what is happening. Allowing them to be involved as much as possible with the family and in preparing for the funeral will make death less frightening, and minimise the chance that their imagination will run wild. Ask them how they want to be involved. Give them options and let them choose.

In certain circumstances such as suicide and homicide, how much detail you tell a child needs to be decided by the child's parents or caregivers. This decision needs to consider the following factors.

- The child's age
- Their understanding of the finality of death
- The nature of the death and whether the information will distress them
- Their relationship to the person who has died
- The amount of contact they had with the person who has died
- Whether they are likely to be told or learn about the death from other sources

---

A good rule of thumb is to tell the facts simply, allowing the child's questioning to dictate how much information you give. Suicide is probably the hardest for a young child to comprehend – even if they hear the word they may not know what it means. As difficult as it might be to tell the truth about the events that led to the death, not telling brings its own set of problems. These include the following.

- Division in the family based on a 'secret'
- A risk that the children will hear from their friends, often in an unkind way
- Losing track of who knows what
- Deciding when to tell the truth and the problems associated with the child finding out the 'secret' at a later date

We were all devastated when my brother committed suicide by walking in front of a train. At the time my son was seven, and even though we felt he was too young to understand depression and suicide, we told him that this happened because his uncle was very sick and wasn't thinking right.

BRONWYN, 32

SUGGESTION: INFORMING THE SCHOOL

When a significant loved one dies and a child will be absent from school for a period of time, designate someone to contact their school. Keep the teacher informed about how the child is reacting and when they will return to school, so that the class can acknowledge the death in an appropriate way. Some teachers ask the other children to make cards telling the child how sorry they were to hear about the death of their loved one. You might also want to tell the school what information you would like shared with other parents and caregivers about the death, so that the teacher can send home a letter. This way you have some control over what is said to others and about who knows what.

Preparing children for the funeral

How much a child should be involved in the funeral probably depends on how close they were to the person who died, and the nature of the relationship. Not that long ago parents were discouraged from taking children to funerals or wakes in case it was too traumatic for them, or they were too disruptive. Now health professionals encourage families to include children – if they want to attend – in the funerals or memorial services of close relatives or friends, so they are a part of the grieving process. It also provides an opportunity for them to learn that death is a normal and expected part of life. Young children may need a 'minder' who can take them out of the service if need be so that their parents do not have to worry about looking after them.

SUGGESTION: ASSIGN A MINDER

It's a good idea before the funeral to ask someone who the child knows well to be prepared to take them out of the service if they become too restless or loud.

If you plan on taking children to a wake or funeral, tell them beforehand what they might expect to see, especially if the coffin or casket will be open. Remember that most young children won't have any experience of funerals and the etiquette associated with such rituals. Explain to them how they are expected to behave. The suggestion over the page will give you some guidance.

Like adults, it's important for children, regardless of their age, to have an opportunity to say goodbye to their loved one. Even if they don't really understand death and its finality, most children have some concept of 'goodbye'. Being able to participate in an activity to say goodbye will help them make some sense of what is happening around them. Ways to do this include saying goodbye to their loved one's body before the funeral service or choosing or making something special to go in the coffin. Here are some suggestions.

- Doing a drawing or painting for their loved one
- Writing a card that they've chosen from the shop
- Making a card
- Writing a letter or poem
- Choosing a special photograph to send with the person. You can then make a copy for the child
- Placing a special toy or trinket in the coffin
- Buying a special flower and placing it on the coffin

Adults might also want to prepare something to go in the coffin. You could choose to prepare these mementos as a family activity, write something privately, or do both. Children will look to the adults in their life for guidance on what to do. Healthy role-modelling about grieving is a wonderful gift to give your children.

If you are reading this book after the funeral and you wished you had written a goodbye letter or card to your loved one, it's not too late. Set aside some time when you can be alone and, using the suggestions above, prepare what you would have liked to have said. You could then take what you've written to the grave or to a special place and read it aloud to your loved one. Alternatively you could keep the letter in a safe place, or burn it and sprinkle the ashes on the grave. It is totally up to you.

SUGGESTIONS FOR PREPARING CHILDREN FOR WAKES OR FUNERALS

Tell the children what to expect in terms that they can understand. Examples include the following.

- _____ will look like they are asleep, but they are actually dead because they are no longer breathing
- _____ will look a little different to how they looked when they were alive
- They will be lying in a large wooden box, which is called a coffin
- They will be wearing_____
- There will be flowers, candles and music playing
- They can no longer hear, see or smell as their heart and brain are not working anymore
- They can no longer feel any pain
- They will feel cold to touch
- People at the wake/funeral/service will be sad and many of them may be crying
- Everyone will be very quiet, which is why we need to be quiet too
- The coffin will be taken to the _____ in a large car, which is called a hearse
- The funeral service will be led by _____ (minister, celebrant, rabbi etc.) and they will talk about _____ and how much we will miss them and the things we will remember about them

CHILDREN'S EXPRESSION OF GRIEF

Children will express their grief differently to adults, and boys will probably express their grief differently to girls. Avoid measuring grief by how much a child cries. Children, unlike adults, are likely to flit in and out of periods of sadness due to their shorter concentration spans and because their understanding of death is far less complex than adults. This is normal and adaptive. Just because they are playing happily with their friends doesn't mean they are not sad or missing their loved one.

When my mother died I was concerned that my 6-year-old son hadn't really cried. They were very close because she lived with us. What my counsellor helped me realise was that his relationship, a generation apart, was different to mine. In his own way he was sad. But he was more concerned at the time that I wasn't going to die next.

PAM, 36

Healthy role-modelling about how to grieve is a wonderful gift to give your children. Seek opportunities to discuss death whenever they arise naturally, such as the changes in season and the death of animals or birds in nature.

Facilitating an ongoing conversation

If your child has suffered a significant loss such as the death of a parent or sibling, it's essential to work out a way to facilitate an ongoing conversation with your child about the death. Doing this helps them to grieve in a healthy way. As awkward as it might be for you, children need parents and adults in their life who can take the lead. Rarely will a child instigate a conversation about the death at a later date: they will not be sure if they should and will worry about upsetting other family members. It's important to try to pre-empt some of their questions and concerns and open up the discussion. Having a number of significant adults who can share this role is valuable for the child. The list on the following page outlines some suggestions for maintaining an ongoing conversation with your child about the death of their other parent or sibling. Creating family rituals to acknowledge the death and the absence of their loved one is also an important part of keeping open the communication channels.

FACILITATING AN ONGOING CONVERSATION ABOUT THE DEATH OF A PARENT OR SIBLING

- Set aside a regular family 'date' with your children to 'check in' about how they are dealing with the death of their parent or sibling
- Visit places that she or he loved

- Find out about upcoming events at school that might be difficult: Mother's Day or Father's Day events; mother/father and child dances; sibling photo days; sports or games days and events; and important school milestones such as graduation ceremonies
- Encourage children to ask questions and share their concerns
- Use a family diary where any family member can write down things that they would like to discuss about how the death is impacting on their life. Discuss any entries at the next scheduled family 'date'
- Promote strong relationships with other family members of the same sex as the parent or sibling who died. Encourage favourite aunts or uncles to take a special interest in the child's development, especially during adolescence
- With any issue the child faces, talk about what their parent/sibling would say if he or she were there now
- Use the deceased's name often when the family is together, to send a clear message that it is okay to continue to talk about them
- Find a support group or grief camp for children where they can meet other children who have experienced similar losses

---

SUGGESTION: SEPARATED OR DIVORCED PARENTS

Even if you were no longer in a relationship with your child's other parent when they died, it is important that you focus on your child and what they have lost with the death of their parent. If your relationship was hostile and you don't think that you can talk constructively about the death of your ex, it would benefit your child if you could find a close friend or relative who could take on this role instead of you.

After my sister died I sought out every opportunity to spend time with my nieces and nephew because their father began a new relationship with another woman almost immediately. I feared that he would not continue to talk about my sister with his kids because of his new girlfriend. Whenever the children visit me I tell them stories about their mum and try to honour her memory in the best way I can.

REBECCA, 38

TEENAGERS

Most teenagers do not want their peers to see them as 'different', so it is very likely your child won't openly discuss the death of their loved one with their friends because they feel embarrassed or awkward. They probably will want things to continue as usual. But teenagers do benefit from speaking to other young people who have experienced the death of a loved one. Finding a bereavement support group for teenagers of a similar age is one way to provide them with the opportunity to discuss their loss. Another way is to create family rituals and traditions that keep their loved one present in their lives, and which allow for the possibility of discussion. Be prepared that teenagers may resist these family rituals and may only participate 'at a distance'.

SUGGESTION: DEALING WITH PUBERTY

If possible, encourage a positive relationship between your children and another family member of the same sex as the parent who died. This helps to fulfil some of what's missing with the death of their parent. Examples include dealing with puberty, dating and career choices.

When my sister died I wanted to be there for my nieces to help with all the girlie stuff. Their dad is great, but I knew that as soon as puberty hit they would need a woman in their lives to talk about periods, boys and sex. We see each other regularly, go out shopping together,

*and do the fun things they would have loved to do with
their mother.*

LORNA, 44

Talking with adults

It is impossible to pre-empt all the difficult conversations
you are likely to have with adults in your life about the
death of your loved one. People will say things that are very
hurtful and catch you totally by surprise, while other comments will be made that you half expected. Unfortunately
many people, even if they are well intentioned, often say
hurtful things because they want to 'fix' you or they lack
the empathy necessary to understand another person's
pain. Typically, difficult conversations fall into two main
categories.

- About the death itself
- Interpretations about your 'progress'

These conversations might catch you off guard, or you
could be the one who initiates them as a result of someone else's comment or action. Again, having a framework
can help you work out how best to prepare or tackle such
conversations.

Preparing for difficult conversations

Depending on the circumstances, you might have to retell the events of the death to many different people including family, friends, colleagues and officials. The more you have these conversations and face people you haven't seen since the death, the easier it will become. Planning what you want to say and writing it down – especially if you need to call someone – will help you feel more in control. Exercise 6.2 gives you some tips on how to make a plan. Sending an email to work colleagues is a good way to tell a number of people the same information. Even though you still have to see them eventually, you will feel more at ease because they already 'know' some of your story.

> *When I returned to work after my husband died, I had to attend an in-house conference where I knew just about everyone. I was anxious about how I would react the first time I saw my colleagues. I didn't want to break down because I feared I wouldn't be able to stay. I decided to email everyone a few days before, thanking them for their condolences and letting them know that I was doing as well as could be expected. People still came up to me, but I felt that I could control the situation better because there had been some contact beforehand.*
>
> JOYCE, 58

SUGGESTION: USE EMAIL

Email can be a great communication tool that allows you to tell a number of people – such as work colleagues – the same information. You can ask someone to communicate with other people on your behalf if you're not up to it.

EXERCISE 6.2: PLAN WHAT TO SAY ABOUT THE DEATH OF YOUR LOVED ONE

You will feel more in control if you plan a simple statement about the death of your loved one that you can repeat to people who are not in your immediate circle of family or friends, when they ask how you are. Write down the answers in steps 1 and 2, and use them to write your statement in step 3.

Step 1. What information would you like them to know?

_____

_____

_____

Step 2. What information would you prefer they didn't know?

_____

_____

_____

Step 3. Write down in a sentence what you would like to say. Rehearse it.

_____

_____

_____

Another difficult conversation you might find yourself needing to have is telling those who care about you that it doesn't help to hear that someone else is worse off than you. You will need to find the words to let the person know that you don't want to hear about these stories now. The following conversation between Joan and Nancy might give you some ideas.

Joan: Nancy, I was really sorry to hear about Jack. What happened?

Nancy: Well, he had been feeling unwell for the last three weeks since having a few chest pains and was having some tests. The doctors were trying him on different medications for angina when he just died in the hospital . . .

Joan: That's awful. That's exactly what happened to my friend's husband - you know Brenda, the one who has the twin granddaughters. Yes, that was very sad. Just the same - a heart attack and so young. A few years younger than Jack, I think. Brenda's not doing well either and it's been two months now.

You can see that this conversation doesn't help Nancy at all. Joan hasn't listened to her, she's cut her off mid-sentence, and has changed the subject to someone else's hardship. Even though it is difficult, Nancy will need to speak up for herself otherwise she runs the risk of Joan telling her about other people's woes every time they speak. Exercise 6.3 shows you how to plan for difficult conversations about the death of your loved one with the adults in your life.

EXERCISE 6.3: FRAMEWORK FOR APPROACHING DIFFICULT CONVERSATIONS

Step 1. Write down the situation that is upsetting you — identify the issue and person you want to talk to.

Step 2. What would you like to say about what was said/done or not said/done? Write it down.

Step 3. What would you like to be different? Make a request and write it down.

Step 4. Rehearse what you would like to say.

Step 5. Arrange a time to speak to the person in question.

Nancy used this framework to plan what she wanted to say to Joan. They met up a few days later and Nancy was able to talk in an assertive manner about what she needed.

Nancy: Joan, I'm sorry to hear about your friend Brenda, but at the moment I am struggling with Jack's death and find it's too painful to hear about other people's grief. I appreciate you calling but I need just to focus on me for the moment. Would you mind not talking about Brenda?

Conversations like this won't be easy, but the situation will only fester if you don't speak up for what you need or want. Thinking too much about what others said or didn't say uses up valuable energy that you need for your grieving. Remember that no one can read your mind so you need to become your best advocate. The same logic applies when people behave in a way contrary to what you expected. Maybe they didn't behave in the way you had hoped – as in Maddie and Jacqui's cases – or they said they would do something but then didn't, as Phil found out.

Soon after my mother died I really wanted to talk about her death with my sister. Whenever I visited, hoping to have an opportunity to talk about our mum, she would always seem to avoid the subject. She seemed to withdraw, whereas I felt a strong need to connect with her about mum and the memories we shared. Eventually, with encouragement from my psychologist, I approached my sister and told her how I felt. I asked her whether we could spend some time together talking about old times. She agreed, reluctantly, and in the end I felt a little better because I was able to express my feelings.

MADDIE, 48

After my partner's death, his estranged brother kept calling me to ask about the will and his estate. I think, because we weren't married, he thought he might have been left something. That wasn't the case – they hadn't seen each other in years. It really bothered me that this guy had the nerve to call and that I had to deal with him when I was struggling with my own pain.

JACQUI, 35

So many people said they would call or visit after my wife died. They haven't. The phone never stopped ringing when she was alive but now it's quiet. I don't know whether I am hurt or angry, but I can't stop thinking about it and I don't think I should be the one to have to call.

PHIL, 68

As hard as it is, it's up to you to decide how you react to what people say or don't say. Many bereaved people say that they really worked out who their true friends were after the death of a loved one. If something is affecting you – if someone has said something that has offended you, or you are disappointed by their behaviour – you need to speak up. Plan what you'd like to say and choose your time using the framework for approaching difficult conversations (exercise 6.3). Always sleep on these types of discussions if time permits because you are likely to be more sensitive than usual when you are grieving.

One of the most hurtful comments was made to me by a good friend, soon after my grandmother died. My friend said, 'She was eighty-nine – you knew that she would die one day. You just have to pull yourself together and get on with things.' What my friend didn't realise was that my grandmother was like a mother to me, and I had cared for her for many years. It didn't matter to me whether she was eighty-nine or one hundred and thirty-nine – all I knew is that I was devastated when she died. There were no words to describe my sense of loss. My friend's comment made it worse. I am angry that she could be so callous and I am not sure whether our relationship can ever be the same again.

LUCY, 37

SUGGESTION: DEALING WITH OTHERS

There are likely to be many times when people do not act in the way you would have hoped. When you are grieving, speaking up in an assertive manner about your needs will help you feel better about the situation, but it is important to accept that the people around you might never behave in the way you would like. If possible, try to sleep on these difficult conversations because you are likely to be more sensitive when your grief is new.

At work

The same strategies can be applied to interacting with your work colleagues. There is no way to predict how they will treat you on your first day back at work – it depends on their experience and comfort level with death. There will, no doubt, be colleagues who say how sorry they are and seem willing to listen, as well as those who awkwardly express their sympathy and walk off quickly. Then there will be those who avoid you like the plague, and sadly there might be those who say nothing at all. In the same way that you can feel let down by family or friends, you might feel disappointed or disheartened by the way your colleagues react. You might feel that your grieving is made even more difficult because you expected something else. Each situation will be different. If you find yourself unhappy with something that someone has said or done, or not said or done, then use the framework in exercise 6.3 to determine how to approach the situation.

> *I returned to work a week after my husband died and my boss couldn't even look me in the eye on the first day. I was so hurt. I expected something quite different, especially because my boss is a woman.*

> MARGIE, 55

> *I just wanted to get back to business as usual. Some colleagues came to the funeral, but after that I didn't really want to talk about it. I told a few of my closest colleagues and I think they spread the word because people left me alone after that.*

> MITCH, 50

Empathy

When people make comments that are hurtful, a lack of empathy is usually the culprit. Empathy is largely misunderstood: contrary to popular belief, it is not about imagining how *you* would think or feel in the given situation. Rather, it is about imagining how someone else feels in the situation they are in. Empathy helps you to understand, as much as you can, another person's pain, hardship or love. It doesn't mean you know how someone else feels because that is impossible. It's about forgetting your own perspective, focusing on someone else's experience, and imagining what life is like for them at that given point in time. Empathy allows you to accept what someone feels as their reality, and doesn't involve telling them how to think, feel or act.

To be truly empathic requires the following.

- To listen really closely to what you are being told
- To resist the urge to offer solutions
- To be comfortable with silence
- To be comfortable with things that are difficult to hear
- To avoid bringing up similar experiences you know of, or have had

If you suspect some of your friends, family or colleagues have little empathy for your situation, you need to protect yourself from being hurt. Keep your expectations realistic about how they will treat you. Empathy is a skill that requires practice. The chances are, your friends and family are well meaning but ill-informed. You may end up weeding out those friends who 'get it' from those who don't. If you are constantly disappointed by someone's reaction, you need to lower your expectations about the type of support they can provide.

When Vicki's partner of fifteen years died, she was very hurt when her best friend told her several months later that she needed to 'get over it'. Vicki had expected that her friend would be able to listen to her pain for some time. She found out that her friend couldn't, so she decided that she needed to go elsewhere for support when she was feeling miserable. By joining a bereavement support group, Vicki made friends with other women whose husbands or partners had died. Even though their circumstances were different, she felt a greater sense of understanding and empathy from these women.

Next steps

Challenging your thoughts, identifying barriers, developing new routines and having difficult conversations are an ongoing part of overcoming your grief. As you continue to move forward on your new path, the focus now is to turn your attention to how best to maintain a connection with your loved one – another important tool. In the next chapter we will look at how you can go about doing this.

Summary

- Children, like adults, grieve in their own way
- Explain the truth about death to children in simple language, appropriate for their developmental age
- Avoid euphemisms as children find them confusing
- Help children find a way to say goodbye to their loved one

- Facilitate ongoing conversations with children and teenagers about their loved one
- Prepare for difficult conversations with children and adults
- Be assertive by speaking up about your needs

7

Maintaining a connection

Many people fear that they will forget their loved one. You might be worrying that you will forget their face, their smell or their touch. Or you may think that you will forget the sound of their voice. All of these fears are normal and a part of reconciling the death of someone significant. It is true that as days turn into months, and months turn into years, it becomes harder to recall these specific characteristics as memories fade. These days technology helps with cameras and smartphones, although smell and touch are obviously more difficult to capture and remember. As well as fears about forgetting your loved one, you might have questions that relate to moving forward. Many people have questions about their loved one's belongings, about whether they should continue to wear their wedding ring, and about moving or selling their home. In this chapter we'll look at these questions and why it's important to turn your attention to what you can do to remember your loved one, rather than worrying about what you might forget.

Common questions

People who are grieving often struggle with many questions in the beginning. You might have already been thinking about some of the following.

Will I forget?

It is very normal, especially in the early months, to worry about forgetting your loved one and not to want to remove anything that signified their life. Being ambivalent about giving away their belongings is normal because these things represent a link between the two of you. It's best not to rush to do anything unless *you* want to, even if your friends and family think you should. Often those around you assume that seeing your loved one's things every day is only making you feel worse, whereas they may actually be bringing you comfort. What people don't understand is that it takes time for your head and your heart to catch up with each other. You *know* that your loved one has died but it's hard to let go of the many things that were so much a part of their life and your life together. Some people think that they are being disloyal if they give away their loved one's belongings 'too soon'. Others find the task too overwhelming in the early months to even know where to begin.

> *I was devastated when my mother died. It was so unex-*
> *pected. She went in for a routine hospital procedure and*
> *ended up dying from complications two days later. A*
> *week after her funeral I found I had a saved voice message*

from her on my mobile phone. It was so wonderful to hear her voice and I kept playing it over and over. I had to keep saving it so it wouldn't be deleted. Is this normal?

JUDY, 28

I've kept a t-shirt that I bought my father years ago when I was in Africa. Each time I consider throwing it out I put it back in my drawer. It's a link to him that I'm not prepared to break, even though he died more than ten years ago.

LAUREN, 36

There are no specific rules about what you should and shouldn't do. Do what feels right for you, even if some of your friends and relatives express concern about whether these things are good for you.

My husband recorded the greeting on our answering machine and my kids want me to change it. I don't want to because listening to his voice makes me think he's still here, whereas they don't like hearing it when they call because they know he's not. I'm sure I will change it at some stage, but not yet.

MARGARET, 57

As a guide, anything is okay if it brings you comfort. If you're concerned about whether you are doing the 'right' thing ask yourself, *Is this really helping me?* If the answer is 'yes', then don't be concerned. If someone else is pressuring you to do something different and you don't want to, you need to tell them that you are doing things your way. As time moves on and you begin to adjust to life without your loved one, you'll probably find that you can make changes. You will also find it easier if you can actively work on developing a new connection with your loved one as a part of your grieving. Chapter 3 discussed the importance of carving out time to grieve. You may now be at a point where you want to work on developing a new connection with your loved one as part of your 'grief time'.

It's important to keep in mind that grief is complex. The physical and emotional bond that you shared with your loved one has been broken, and it will take time and effort on your part to develop a new connection with them based on memory and legacy. Naturally it will be different from the old one, but this important step will help you adjust to living without them. Try not to fight it – instead, actively work on defining this new connection.

If you are concerned about whether you are doing the
'right' thing, ask yourself, Is this really helping me?

When is the best time to sort through my loved one's belongings?

If this responsibility lies with you, you need to decide when you're ready – emotionally – to sort through your loved one's belongings. Often well-meaning friends or family, who erroneously believe that 'out of sight is out of mind', will tell you that you need to throw out your loved one's belongings as soon as possible. They might also offer to come and 'assist' you, believing that you will feel better once the task is complete. While this may be the case for some people, others will find comfort in having these personal things around them for a while longer. If you were the one closest to the person who died, try to be present to sort through their belongings – the 'sorting' process provides another opportunity to grieve, sad as it can be to throw things out or give them away. For this reason friends and family should be discouraged from sorting through belongings without the 'primary' bereaved person/people. You will find some helpful suggestions on how to tackle this process in the list below. Different items of clothing or keepsakes can trigger memories that allow you to reminisce and remember your loved one. You need to remind yourself again and again that being sad isn't a bad thing – it is a healthy part of expressing your grief.

GUIDELINES FOR SORTING THROUGH BELONGINGS

- Allow the 'primary' bereaved person/people to dictate the timing
- Begin with things that are the least sentimental or the easiest to sort
- Sort in sections, such as a room or a cupboard at a time

- Allow yourself as much time as you need to go through things
- Allow yourself to cry
- Don't throw out anything if you're unsure. Put it back or store it elsewhere in the house and consider it at a later time
- Select an organisation or charity to which you would like to donate the belongings. Choose one that is meaningful to you or your loved one
- Be prepared to experience 'trigger waves' (see Chapter 2) when you come across various items, especially those that have great sentimental value

I found it very difficult to sort through my husband's personal belongings. For several months I left everything on his bedside table, just as it was the day he died. One day, out of the blue, it dawned on me that his toothbrush was still in the bathroom where it always had been. I surprised myself by just tossing it out. I couldn't have done it early on.

RUTH, 62

Should I take off my wedding ring?

There is no right or wrong answer to this question. Rings have different meanings to different people. Some people take off their ring immediately whereas others vow that they will never remove it. Others decide to leave on their wedding ring until there is a reason to take it off. Only you can decide what is best for you. It's often the case that other family members or friends are more bothered by rings being taken off 'too early' or left on for 'too long'. It's important to ask yourself, *What do I want to do?* If other people are giving you advice or pressuring you one way or the other, then speak up for what you want or tell them that the decision is yours alone. Don't be swayed. You also might have questions about your loved one's rings following their death. Some people give them to a relative, wear them on a chain, or reset them. If there is family conflict you might want to let things settle down before making a decision. If you're trying to decide about something, use the framework for making difficult decisions (exercise 5.2). This can help you make an informed decision about any issue that is bothering you.

> *I kept my wedding ring on after my husband died. In my mind we were still married – there was never a decision to make about whether to take it off. I gave our son his father's wedding ring when he got married, which was really special for all of us.*
>
> ABBY, 54

If others are pressuring you, don't be afraid to speak up for what you want to do.

How often should I visit the cemetery?

Again there is no simple answer to this question. Use your emotions as your barometer. If you come away from the cemetery feeling comforted, then for now you might decide to continue visiting as often as you do. But if you feel worse each time it might be best to reduce the frequency of your visits and identify the thoughts that are triggering your emotions (see exercise 4.5). Some people, for example, report that they feel tremendous guilt if they don't visit the cemetery often, whereas others visit only rarely and are fine with their decision. If you believe that your reason for visiting the cemetery is to avoid guilt then, as you did in exercise 4.5, challenge your thinking, because this is a barrier that you will want to overcome. Ask yourself, *What would my loved one tell me to do?* Most people eventually fall into a pattern that suits them. As you move forward in your grief it is realistic to expect that you will feel the need to visit the cemetery less often than you did in the beginning.

SUGGESTION: BEWARE OF THE 'SHOULDS'

If you find that you use the word 'should' a lot in relation to what you think you should or shouldn't be doing then let warning bells sound. 'Should' statements imply that you must do something otherwise you are doing the wrong thing, and they are usually associated with guilt, resentment or anger.

To sell or not to sell?

Whether to sell, move or renovate are common questions that people ask early on. Often people just want to get away and escape the painful memories. For others it comes down to finances and whether or not they can maintain their home. As with all of these issues there is no one correct answer. You need to focus on weighing up the reasons for and against making any decision and be aware of the consequences. The framework for making difficult decisions (exercise 5.2) will help you do this.

If you've recently experienced the death of a loved one and want some general guidance, most health professionals recommend waiting at least twelve months if possible before making an irreversible decision such as selling a house. There will be exceptions but this is good advice because it allows time for your waves of grief to lessen in intensity and frequency. Waiting also helps minimise change in your life. Once you begin to adjust to life without your loved one, you will be less likely to make a decision based on emotion and more able to focus on the facts.

After our daughter died we thought about moving because it was just too hard to stay in the house without her. Her brothers and sister didn't want to be there with her empty bedroom. We decided to give it a year and we changed the rooms around so it was a little different. It did help, but two years later we went ahead with the move. In a way it signalled a new beginning for us.

VICTORIA, 44

*Before my wife died we were talking about selling up
and moving into a smaller house – our family home had
become too much for both of us. Even though it will be
hard to leave this old house and all its memories, I know
she would want me to.*

EARL, 71

Let's look at an example using the framework for making
difficult decisions. Three months ago Judith's husband died
suddenly. Her adult children live several hundred miles away
and want her to sell up and move closer to them because
she can no longer manage the upkeep on the house. Judith
is finding this decision very difficult – moving means selling
the family home that she and her husband shared for nearly
forty years, and leaving behind the memories of their life
together. Judith's responses are shown below.

FRAMEWORK FOR MAKING DIFFICULT DECISIONS, JUDITH'S ANSWERS

Step 1. What is the problem you are experiencing
or the decision you are facing?

*Whether to sell my house and move closer to my
children or stay where I am.*

Step 2. How many possible solutions can you list?

1. Sell and move closer to my children.

---

2. Stay where I am.

3. Sell and find something smaller here.

Step 3. What are the positives and negatives of each of these possible solutions?

1. Sell and move closer to my children.

+ Would be near my children and grandchildren; not so lonely; cheaper; have help.

– Leaving my home and its memories.

2. Stay where I am.

+ Love my house; memories; connection to my husband.

– Big; old house; can't afford the maintenance; can't physically manage the garden.

3. Sell and find something smaller here.

+ Stay in the same town.

– Selling my home and leaving its memories; being a long way from my children and grandchildren.

Step 4. Which looks best to you?

1. Sell and move closer to my children.

Step 5. If you used this solution, what would the consequences be?

I could never come back to my house as I know it now.

Step 6. Can you live with these consequences? Yes/No

Yes, but it will be very hard. Maybe if I wait for a few more months – perhaps until the spring – I will feel more able to leave.

Step 7. If you answered 'no' in step 6, go back to step 2 and work through the remaining steps again.

Step 8. If you used the solution outlined in step 4, what action do you need to take to try out this solution?

1. *Visit my children for a few weeks and get to know the area a little better.*
2. *Look at houses or apartments to either rent or buy that will suit some of the furniture we bought together over the years.*
3. *Tell my children I will wait until the spring to put my house on the market and move.*

Judith knew deep down that moving was the best decision for her, given her circumstances. But working through her decision in this way made it a very deliberate choice. In the end she was able to agree that she could live with the consequences of moving but decided that she needed to do some preparation to give her plan the best chance of success. In step 8 she listed visiting her children and looking at properties as things she needed to do before putting her house on the market. She also decided that in choosing a new home, she would make sure that she had room for a number of the sentimental pieces of furniture that she and her husband had bought together over the years. Judith also was able to reason that if she waited a few months until the spring, leaving her home might be a little easier than it would be now.

EXERCISE 7.1: MAKING DIFFICULT DECISIONS

Are you currently facing any difficult decisions concerning your life? These might be decisions specifically about your loved one's death or about how to move forward with your life. Like Judith did, use the framework for making difficult decisions to help work through your options. You will find a blank framework in Appendix 2.

Maintaining a connection with your loved one

When the initial shock of a loved one's death wears off and life begins slowly to return to something of what it used to be, many people turn their attention to developing a new connection with the person who died. This involves working out how you are going to continue to have a relationship with them now they are no longer physically here. This might sound a little odd, but the aim of overcoming your grief isn't to forget your loved one but to learn to live without them physically in your life. So in essence the connection you had with them has changed, not ceased. Working out what this new connection will look like won't happen overnight. Eventually, most people who are grieving get to a point where they can invest emotionally in developing a new and different connection with their loved one.

The following set of questions, as listed in Exercise 7.2, can help you think about how to develop a new connection with your loved one that is now based on memory and legacy.

1. Who were they to you?

The answer to this question involves so much more than just stating the nature of the relationship you shared with your loved one. The person who died might have been your parent, child, partner or friend, but they may also have represented so many other things. Perhaps they were your advocate, your confidant or your dreams. Or maybe they were simply the one who was always there for you.

2. What did you learn from them?

This probably is the most important component of working

out how to maintain a connection with your loved one. When people touch our lives – even if it's only for a very short time – it changes who we are. We learn things about ourselves that maybe we didn't know before. We also change as a result of their death and the adjustments we need to make in our lives.

3. What values did they impart to you?

Did your loved one have any specific values that you have taken on? This is a particularly helpful question for young adults whose parent has died.

4. What were they passionate about in life?

Answering this question may give you some ideas about where you might want to direct some of your time and energy in their memory.

5. What history do you share?

The shared history with your loved one is something that can never be taken away. Part of maintaining a connection requires recalling events from the times you spent together. How did you meet? What significant moments did you share?

6. How would they like to be remembered?

When we know someone well we gain a sense of what's important to them, and of who they are and the life they lead. What qualities or attributes would your loved one want you to remember?

7. What would they say to you now?

If your loved one was sitting opposite you now, what would they say about maintaining a connection with them – what suggestions might they have for you? Use exercise 7.2 to explore some of the possibilities.

EXERCISE 7.2: DEVELOPING A NEW CONNECTION

You've probably been thinking about your answers already as you read through the explanations of the seven questions. Now, in your journal, answer the following questions about your loved one. Begin by jotting down phrases or key points. Add to them later as you think of other things.

1. Who were they to you?
2. What did you learn from them?
3. What values did they impart to you?
4. What were they passionate about in life?
5. What history do you share?
6. How would they like to be remembered?
7. What would they say to you now?

Nearly seven years ago I lost my father to cancer and heart disease. His death wasn't sudden but he was a huge part of my youth and to this day still influences and affects my life decisions. After the first week of open and constant grieving I began to acknowledge and seek a strength and guidance, which I can only explain as the ingrained influence that Dad had on me. A week after his death I gave up cigarettes, began to talk openly to my mum and really started to take responsibility for the everyday decisions that determine the happiness and passions that now dictate my life. In a way I suppose I took the strength of Dad's convictions, which he always preached throughout my life, and implemented them after he passed on. I was definitely 'Dad's boy' throughout my childhood. Even to this day I shed a tear for the old fella when I think about him, or when I describe his character to my girlfriend. But I take great strength in knowing that although he is not here in person, he lives within me.

JOHN, 34

Tell their story

People often find it helpful to tell the story of the person who has died – it helps them overcome their grief by keeping their loved one's memory alive. You often see this when someone dies tragically and the survivors take up a cause as a part of going on themselves. For example, you may see public figures turning their time and attention to fundraising and increasing public awareness about certain illnesses following the death of a loved one. In criminal cases, often the only way for family members to go on is to try to make sure that the same horrible death doesn't happen to some-one else.

Regardless of who in your life died, you may want to tell their life story and talk about the impact they had on others. If their death was sudden and unexpected this will be an important part of working out how you go about developing a new connection with them. When children, young adults or young parents die, it's essential for those left behind to maintain a connection because they wouldn't have anticipated losing their loved one at such a young age.

REMEMBERING YOUR LOVED ONE

Many people who are grieving find it difficult – especially in the early months – to remember their loved one as they were in happy times. Instead, the memories that are most prominent are those of their loved one's last days, perhaps when they were very ill or after they had died. Being able to remember them as they were is something you can actively work on. Exercise 7.3 will show you how.

EXERCISE 7.3: REMEMBERING YOUR LOVED ONE WITH A SMILE

For some people, memories of their loved one in happy times can be tainted by memories of their loved one's final days. These seven steps will help you to actively focus on the positive memories to redress this imbalance. For each of the steps note down in your journal whatever comes to mind.

Step 1. Write a description of the memories that are troubling you.

Step 2. Now think back to a happy time. What were you doing? How old was your loved one?

Step 3. Select another memory. If you are having difficulty thinking of one, look through photos to prompt your memory.

Step 4. Depending on how old your loved one was, think through different decades of their life and write about how you remember them at each point in time.

Step 5. Think over your most recent holidays together. Where did you go? What were the highlights? What did your loved one enjoy most?

Step 6. How did you meet your loved one? What is your first memory of them?

Step 7. Describe your loved one's personality. What characteristics defined who they were?

No one had prepared me for how he would look when I saw him in the morgue. He was lying there in his regular clothes, but the paramedics who worked on him at the scene of the accident had intubated him. He had this big tube in his mouth which apparently could not be removed until the medical examiner gave permission. For a number of weeks that image of him haunted me — it was the last thing I saw before I went to bed each night.

TAYLOR, 33

At 23 I was on track in life. I wasn't thinking beyond my next assignment or exam, or the next party I was going to. Then my father was diagnosed with terminal cancer and he died three months later. During those final months life as I knew it stopped. Every free moment was spent with my family. It was a very special time, full of opportunities to express love and expectations, and to receive guidance. If Dad's pain and suffering hadn't increased continually, I could have lived by his bedside suspended in time forever. But time cannot be frozen, which I now realise is a good thing because then I would still be trapped in the overwhelming grief I felt after he was gone. Seventeen years later I can still imagine what he would be saying to me, how he would have loved his grandchildren and how he would still be loving my mum. I may have lost him in person but he has never left my mind or heart.

JO, 41

CREATING A 'MEMORY BOOK'

Many people who are grieving find it very therapeutic to make a memory or photo book that tells their loved one's story. It can be something private that you do on your own or you can involve others, which can benefit them too if they're also grieving for your loved one. Not only is this a wonderful exercise in allowing you to move through your grief, but it also helps you to maintain a connection with your loved one and guards against the fear of forgetting them. Many people find this a difficult task, but on completing it they say that they are so glad they did it. As you begin to create your memory book it will help if you try to embrace the memories rather than fight them. And remember to give yourself permission to cry.

You can make the memory book for your own use, and in doing so become the keeper of your loved one's story. Or you can make the book to give as a gift to others, such as younger family members. With today's technology and online applications you can easily make multiple copies.

There are many ways to create a memory book. Exercise 7.4 will give you some suggestions about making a traditional scrapbook. You can also scan and upload photos to make an online photo book. It's important to do whatever is most meaningful to you.

EXERCISE 7.4: CREATING A MEMORY BOOK

Step 1. Buy a large scrapbook or photo album that has meaning to you – maybe it's a certain colour or has a picture on the cover that reminds you of your loved one.

Step 2. Use a large box to collect any mementos so you can store the items as you go. That way you'll have all the keepsakes in a safe place if you don't want to start making the book right away.

Step 3. Collect anything that is important to you and which tells a part of your loved one's story. Examples include birthday, anniversary, and sympathy cards; photos from different events or time periods; the obituary cutting from the newspaper; or the order of service from the funeral. You might want to make copies rather than using the originals in the book.

Step 4. Send out a group email to your friends and family asking them to write a paragraph or two about their fondest memories of your loved one, or about how they met or what they learned from them. This is a wonderful way to find out more about your loved one's life, and it's especially valuable if there are young children who will one day want to know more about the person who died.

Step 5. Think about the things that were meaningful to your loved one and include lists of their favourite sayings or pastimes, their favourite music, food, restaurants, movies and so on.

Step 6. When you've collected everything you need and you're ready to begin, you can start to arrange the order and layout. You may not have the energy to do this for some time, which is why gathering the mementos in a box is a good strategy.

Step 7. When it comes to making the memory book, you can either do this on your own or ask other family members or friends to help.

TIPS FOR ASKING OTHERS FOR INFORMATION AND STORIES

These questions can be good for gathering information about your loved one to put in your memory book.

- How did you meet _____?
- How long have you known _____?
- What are your first memories of _____?
- What are your fondest memories of _____?
- What are your funniest stories of _____?
- What qualities did you value in _____?
- How do you think _____ would like to be remembered?

SUGGESTION: ENCOURAGE CHILDREN TO MAKE THEIR OWN MEMORY BOOK

Children of all ages can be involved in making their own memory or photo book, which not only helps them to express their feelings but also allows them to maintain a connection with their loved one. Depending on their age, they can be involved in selecting the photos that are special to them, drawing pictures and writing about the person who died.

These suggestions may be useful if they need help getting started with their writing: I remember when we . . ., I feel . . ., I wish I could tell you . . ., I love you because . . .

Other ways to maintain a connection

There are many other ways to maintain a connection to your loved one. You could try some of the ones listed here or you could use your grief time (see Chapter 3) to think about activities that would be meaningful to you.

- Plant your loved one's favourite flowers each year
- Donate or plant a tree
- Support a significant cause
- Make a DVD compilation of old home movies
- Make a playlist of their favourite songs
- Use their old clothes to make something of significance such as pyjamas, cushions, pillow cases or a patchwork quilt
- Invite others to contribute stories about your loved one that you can compile in a book or album

- Make a special photo book of your favourite photos using an online application
- Enlarge a favourite photo and have it framed
- Redecorate a room in a way that reminds you of your loved one
- Visit places that were special to both of you
- Continue to share your loved one's stories, jokes and favourite sayings
- Spend time in nature, where you can think about your loved one
- Celebrate their birthday
- Walk or run in their memory at a fundraiser for a local charity

My father fought off death many times. We were all prepared when he finally died after years of being sick. He would joke, 'Don't buy me a new shirt, I have enough to see me out.' On many occasions I thanked him for being a great dad and he often said, 'Look after your mother.' I was able to write him a thank you letter several months before his death and I was there when he died. Of course every life and death is unique. But from my experience with Dad I'd say these four things.

1. ***We were very fortunate to be able to prepare for his death**. My father-in-law died suddenly – there was no warning and no opportunity for the family to*

say goodbye. He was healthy one day and dead the next. My dad's death was a complete contrast.

2. **At the same time, I hope I die a more sudden death**. It's tough watching someone you love get progressively worse to the point that their life has little dignity left. While I'm thankful Dad lived every extra day he did, I hope I don't have a drawn-out death for my family.

3. **We all should make the right choices to keep as healthy as possible**. I often wonder whether my father would have lived to spend more time with us if he had made better health choices. He was always a heavy smoker until his first heart attack at the age of 42. To his credit he gave up smoking after this first brush with death.

4. **Death is not the end**. My family still laughs with Dad on a regular basis. We recall his jokes, the family stories, and what he would have said. I certainly still feel very connected with him. Dad loved the outdoors. A little over a year after he died I discovered a lake in a part of the world my dad never had the opportunity to visit. I connect with Dad at this lake on a regular basis. I call the lake 'Heaven' both because of its serenity and beauty, and because of its connection with Dad.

HEDLEY, 46

When the parent of a young child dies

When a young child experiences the death of a parent, other family members need to assume the responsibility of creating and maintaining a connection between the parent and child. This can be done on many different levels including gathering photos, writing stories, and making memory books. Many people with children record messages and stories when they know they are terminally ill. Even though this is very hard to do, they are comforted by the fact that they can leave behind something of themselves for their children to watch after their death. It's also important to create family traditions around holidays and other significant events that acknowledge the person who has died. These will be discussed in the next chapter. Here's a list of suggestions for maintaining a child's connection with their loved one.

- Ask family and friends to write down their memories
- Create a memory book for the child/children
- Encourage the surviving parent to write about their life together. This could include how they met, what attracted them to each other, what they enjoyed doing together, and what they believe the other parent would want for their child/children
- Create a special compilation DVD of happy times

- Help the child/children to make their own memory book including special photos, drawings, and their own story about the death of their loved one

My daughter Carla died four months after her first baby was born. She had been diagnosed with cancer several years before, but it came back during her pregnancy. She was such a fun-loving and vibrant person – everybody loved her. I wanted her daughter one day to know the kind of person she was. So shortly after her death I made it my mission to start a memory book that would tell her story. First I contacted all her friends and our family via email, and asked them to write about why they loved Carla and what they remember about her. Next I collected photos and other mementos from the three different decades of her life. With her husband's help I wrote down the messages I knew she would want her daughter to hear as she grew up. Luckily Carla recorded some of her life story on video for her daughter before she died. Finally, I wrote my own words about Carla. I wrote about her birth and what she was like growing up, and then her husband wrote about how they had met and their years together. The whole book took me nearly two years to complete. At times it was so hard, but I never wanted to quit because I wanted my daughter's memory to be passed on to her daughter. My granddaughter is now three and loves to look at the book and talk about her mummy.

Gwen, 67

The death of a child

When a young child dies, not only is their life cut short but so are the parents' hopes and dreams for their future. It can be very difficult to maintain a connection, especially if the child died at a very young age, because there would have been little opportunity to create shared memories.

Here are some suggestions for parents trying to maintain a connection with their child.

- Ask friends and family to write about their memories of your child
- Ask your child's classmates to write or make something in their memory
- Create a memory book
- Write your child's story
- Write about the hopes you had for your child – what did you think they would do when they grew up?
- Support a cause in their memory
- Create a DVD

When a baby is stillborn it is vital for the parents to be able to grieve openly and to develop a connection with their baby. This is why parents are encouraged to spend time with their baby after the delivery. They can hold and dress the baby, take photos, and make prints of their hands and feet. These mementos can be used to make a memory book along with photos taken through the pregnancy, ultrasound images, the baby's name tag and other memorabilia. It is also important for parents to be able to grieve the death of a baby miscarried earlier in pregnancy, and this can be done in a similar way.

When my baby was stillborn I felt I couldn't talk about her to anyone. No one knew what to say and many of my friends had babies of their own and felt awkward around me. I ended up becoming very depressed and sought help from a psychologist. She encouraged me to tell my own story and my daughter's. I realised it was so hard for everyone because I had had a relationship with my child for nine months whereas they hadn't. I made a memory book and started to talk about her with my friends and family. In doing this she became a part of our lives and we were able to grieve.

TANYA, 34

SUGGESTION: LET OTHERS KNOW

People often don't know what to say or how to respond to you if you're grieving, so tell the significant people in your life what you would like them to do. Maybe you would like them to call, or to talk about your loved one using their name, or simply just to give you a hug. If you don't speak up about what you want or need, they won't know how to comfort you.

Continuing on

Working out the connection that is right for you will take time. As it evolves you may need to try different things. And if you can share your grief with other family members, then together you can create meaningful traditions to honour and remember your loved one. As you continue to work towards overcoming your grief you will hopefully get to a point where you can accept that your loved one isn't here anymore and that your life has changed. Of course you'll wish that they were still here with you, but eventually you will be able to recall memories without the intense pain you experienced in the beginning. It will be as though you've turned down the volume of your grief – like turning down your stereo. The next chapter will give you some strategies to deal with the 'firsts' you'll experience in the days, weeks and months following your loved one's death.

Summary

- There are no fixed rules about what you should or shouldn't do when you are grieving
- Consider all the options and consequences if you're facing a difficult decision
- Work towards developing a connection with your loved one that is based on memory and legacy
- Tell your loved one's story

8

The 'firsts'

How many 'firsts' have you already encountered since your
loved one died? While most people expect that the first
anniversary of the death will be difficult, many don't realise the impact that all the other firsts can have on them.
You may have anticipated that spending the first birthday
or wedding anniversary without your loved one would be
painful, but other events might have caught you by surprise.
Perhaps it was the first time you heard a special song on the
radio, or when you drove past a favourite restaurant and
remembered the last time you were there together. Each
one can affect you differently. In this chapter you'll learn
how to get through each first. Being able to face these firsts
is an important part of adjusting to your life without the
person who died. There are four key components to doing
this: anticipating the first, planning ahead, developing realistic expectations and reminiscing. These form the basis of
the framework for tackling firsts, which will be introduced
later in the chapter.

The first year

The death of one person brings many, many changes to the lives of those left behind. The number of changes you experience is a good predictor of the number of firsts you will have to endure. The list of firsts is endless and is different for everyone. Quite often a first will correlate with a trigger wave on your overall wave-like pattern of grief and you may notice an increased sense of yearning for your loved one. Some events will result in stronger waves than others. Listed below are a number of firsts that people commonly report. Just being aware that these events may be painful firsts can help you prepare for them ahead of time and develop a plan.

COMMON EXAMPLES OF 'FIRSTS'

ILLNESS AND DEATH

- The date the illness was diagnosed
- The first anniversary of the death
- Seeing something on television that relates to your loved one's illness or death
- When the date and day of a month are the same as the date and day of the death

PERSONAL BUSINESS

- Visiting the bank

- Using a cash machine
- Filling your car with petrol
- Consulting a lawyer or financial advisor
- Doing odd jobs around the house that your loved one did
- Going to your place of worship
- Meeting acquaintances who ask about your loved one
- Returning to work
- Shopping without your loved one for the first time
- Paying bills

FAMILY AFFAIRS

- Family events such as birthdays, weddings, births, graduations and funerals
- Going on a holiday/vacation

FRIENDSHIPS

- Seeing your loved one's friends, colleagues or classmates
- Friends asking you to go out with them for the first time, on your own

YOUR LOVED ONE

- Your loved one's birthday
- Visiting the cemetery

- Seeing the headstone for the first time
- Eating their favourite food
- Receiving a letter addressed to the person who died
- Watching your loved one's favourite sporting team
- Seeing the same make and colour of your loved one's car
- Seeing other people who remind you of your loved one

YOUR LIFE TOGETHER

- Your wedding anniversary or other significant anniversary
- Your own birthday
- Going to the cinema
- Going out with friends
- Religious holidays
- National holidays
- Sending and receiving Christmas and other seasonal or greetings cards
- The change of season

Now complete exercise 8.1 to examine your own firsts.

EXERCISE 8.1: WHAT FIRSTS HAVE YOU ALREADY EXPERIENCED?

Understanding the impact of firsts can help you prepare better for other events you may be facing without your loved one. Work through the following questions using your journal to record your thoughts.

1. What firsts have you already experienced since your loved one died?
2. Which of them caught you by surprise?
3. Did you do anything to help you get through the day?

My mother died on a Tuesday and it was the tenth of the month. It took many years before I stopped registering when it was a Tuesday and the tenth of the month.

KATHRYN, 41

It is easy to see why grief cannot be over and done with in a matter of weeks when you think about all the firsts in the year following the death. It is fair to say that until you have experienced the first anniversary of your loved one's death, you don't know what first encounters lie ahead. There will always be other firsts in later years but, as time goes on, most people find that they develop a way of coping with these firsts and the impact is not as great as it was in the beginning.

*Planning how to approach firsts will help
you to feel more in control.*

A framework for tackling firsts

Like any issue, using a general framework to tackle firsts will increase your sense of control. There will of course be some firsts that come out of the blue, but you will know when many of them are coming. Trying not to think about them is like trying to ignore the proverbial elephant in the room – it's impossible. It is also important to remind yourself that feeling sad about the first time you face something on your own is not a sign of weakness or a sign that you are getting worse. Remember, pining or yearning for your loved one and feeling sad are expected reactions to their death, and each first is a blatant reminder of their absence and your loss.

As mentioned at the beginning of this chapter, the framework for tackling firsts includes four components: anticipation, planning, realistic expectations and reminiscing.

1. Anticipation

As with most unpleasant or feared events, often the anticipation is worse than the event itself. This is commonly referred to as 'anticipatory anxiety'. Think about the last time you went to the dentist for a procedure. Was it as bad as you imagined beforehand? When you know you have to experience or endure something unpleasant, worrying about it ahead of time usually makes it worse – your mind can run wild, conjuring up all sorts of possibilities. You often fear the worst and the longer you have to wait, the more anxious you become. People usually feel less anxious once the procedure is under way because they have a greater sense of control, especially as they know the end is in sight. And afterwards, most people also report that it wasn't as bad as they'd expected.

To tackle the anticipation factor head on, it's a good idea to make plans for dealing with any predictable first. This will help you feel more in control and help you get through the event.

2. Planning

Developing plans, no matter how simple they are, will make it easier to face events when you are grieving. The first you are concerned about may be a date that signified a happy occasion such as the birth of a child, a birthday or anniversary. Or it may mark a difficult time such as the date when you received the news of a diagnosis, or when you or your loved one decided to cease medical treatment. Whenever a significant date is approaching, think about the following questions as you make your plans.

- What would you like to do to acknowledge the date?
- Is there someone you would like be with on that day?
- Is there anything specific you want to do?
- If the event is a celebration or a family gathering, do you want to do anything differently – for instance celebrate at home together if you usually go to a restaurant?
- What arrangements do you need to make ahead of time?
- How can you carve out time just to be with your grief?

This time a year ago things were going really well for us. We were excited because we had just booked an overseas trip. My wife was scheduled for routine surgery in August and then we were going away in September. I will never forget that day, 18 August, when the surgeon told us that he had found a growth. Now the anniversary of that date is fast approaching for the first time since she died, and I'm dreading the day. I don't know what to do.

CARL, 65

My father died suddenly, two weeks before my birthday. The whole family always spent birthdays together, so we decided to go through the motions even though none of us felt like celebrating – especially me. We picked a favourite restaurant and made it the best evening it could be given the circumstances. It was sad and we all felt Dad's absence, but it certainly got easier each time we got together. It was good to get the first family birthday over and done with. There was an urgency just to 'tick it off'.

GILL, 31

3. Develop realistic expectations

Regardless of which first you're facing, it's important to develop realistic expectations about the day. You might experience a variety of emotions including intense sadness, yearning, anger or guilt during the preceding days and on the day itself. It is totally normal to feel flat or down and have little motivation to do anything. Each first is an acknowledgement of your loss and of the void that has been created by the death of your loved one. Don't set yourself up for more sadness and disappointment by over-committing yourself or expecting that you *should* be able to do this or that. Keep in mind that each first you experience potentially triggers a large wave of grief, the intensity of which may prompt you to question whether you are getting worse again. There will of course be some firsts that affect you less and pass relatively easily. And the more firsts you experience of a similar kind, the easier they will become to tackle.

4. Reminiscing

A large part of overcoming grief involves finding ways to incorporate memories of your loved one and what they meant to you, into your life as it is now. A shift needs to occur – one that enables you to go from living with them physically in your life to living with them only in your memory, at a cognitive and an emotional level. This shift is a process and it won't necessarily happen quickly, although it might happen more easily for some people than others. A lot has to do with how you view life and death, and the relationship you had with the person who died. If they had been ill for a long time before they died, this shift may have already started to occur prior to their death. With degenerative illnesses such as Alzheimer's disease, the person you once knew may have disappeared some time ago and you might have already started to find ways to remember them as they were. If the death was sudden or 'out of order', as with the death of a child, this shift may take a very long time.

Reminiscing, both privately or with others, allows you to access fond memories and helps you to maintain a connection with your loved one. Reminiscing helps you acknowledge who they were and what they meant to you, and highlights opportunities for creating new traditions in their memory.

Reminiscing allows you to access fond memories that help you maintain a connection with your loved one.

Our dad loved a good joke, especially those of the 'vulgar variety'. A visit to our parents' home was never complete without hearing Dad's latest joke. Now, whenever my brothers hear a good joke that Dad might have liked, they immediately email it to the rest of the family. It feels as if we keep in touch with Dad this way and keep him present in our lives.

CLARE, 36

EXERCISE 8.2 WHICH FIRSTS ARE APPROACHING?

It will help you feel more in control if you know ahead of time which firsts to expect. Using your journal, make a list of the firsts that you know are coming up in the next few months.

The first anniversary of the death

The first anniversary of the death of your loved one is probably the one that you fear the most. Irrespective of whether a loved one's death was expected or sudden, people tend to find themselves thinking several weeks beforehand about the first anniversary and how they will get through it. Typical thoughts include, *This time last year we were . . .* and, *If only we'd known this . . .* It is not uncommon to experience a reaction similar to the one you experienced a year ago, just after their death. You may have trouble sleeping again, difficulty eating, or you may find that you cry more readily or frequently. You may feel disappointed with yourself – that you thought you were doing 'better' and now you feel worse again. If you *expect* the first anniversary to be difficult, you'll be less likely to be critical of yourself. It's important to check your thinking and your 'self-talk'. You need to challenge your thinking if you hear yourself saying, *I should be stronger than this*, or, *It's hopeless – I'm never going to feel better*. It's far more helpful to think, *It is normal to feel 'worse' around the time of the first anniversary as I'm thinking back over the events of a year ago. This is all part of grieving and adjusting to my life without my loved one*.

> *As the first anniversary of my six-month-old son's death approached, I couldn't stop asking myself: 'If only…', It was like torture as I went over and over in my mind the events of the days before his death. It did ease but I found it an incredibly difficult period.*
>
> ISABELLE, 32

As outlined in Chapter 2, the first anniversary is likely to trigger a significant wave on your continuous wave-like pattern of grief. You may notice that this wave is larger than the other trigger waves you'd experienced previously. But many people report that they feel a great sense of relief after the first anniversary has passed because they were able to get through it and know that they have now experienced most of their firsts. It's also common for people to say they feel a sense of comfort as they realise they are in a different place than they were a year ago, and can acknowledge that their pain is less intense than it was before.

> *I was overseas on a business trip when it was the first anniversary of my mother's death. I knew I wanted to acknowledge the date, but being in a foreign country made it a little harder. I ended up finding a beautiful church that happened to be open, and I went in and talked to her. Even though I'm not religious, there was something peaceful and serene about the place. I then walked around the grounds and thought about all the things she had taught me during my life. It was a much better day than I had imagined.*
>
> SARA, 28

If the first anniversary of your loved one's death is approaching, complete exercise 8.3 to help you plan ahead for this day. You can also use this exercise to plan for other firsts that might be coming up – look at the list you wrote down in exercise 8.2.

EXERCISE 8.3: THE FIRST ANNIVERSARY

You need to consider each of the four components in the framework for tackling firsts. Work through each of the steps and draw up a plan in your journal that will help you acknowledge the first anniversary of the death of your loved one.

Step 1.   *Anticipation* What is the date of the first anniversary?
Where will you be?

Step 2.   *Planning* Who do you want to be with? What do you want to do?

Step 3.   *Realistic expectations* Look back at the goals you set in step 2. Are these goals realistic? Don't over-commit yourself.

Step 4.   *Reminiscing* What are your favourite memories? Who can you share these with?

I had been going to counselling for a few months before the first anniversary of my husband's death. I knew it was going to be really tough so I wanted to work out how best to get through it, especially as I had my two children to consider. The three of us planned a busy day of visiting. We started at the grave and said our hellos, then we went out to lunch at his favourite restaurant and walked along the beach; finally we went to his mother's house for dinner. Visiting the places that he had always enjoyed allowed us to talk about the good times. We think we will do it again next year.

SANDRA, 58

I was very close to my mother-in-law. When she died there was a huge hole in the family — she had always been the one to bring us together. When her first anniversary was approaching I decided that I would be the one to organise a dinner in her honour. She loved to cook so we all prepared her favourite dishes and got together. I asked everyone to bring a few special photos to share and we spent the evening watching home movies and reminiscing. It was a wonderful tribute to her and everyone was really glad that they came, even though some of the family was a little unsure in the beginning.

ELLA, 27

The first festive holiday season

Christmas, Chanukah, Thanksgiving and other religious or festive holidays where families gather together can be very difficult after the death of someone special. What were once happy and exciting times may now fill you with heartache, anxiety and dread. You might have many mixed emotions and there may be differing opinions between family members about how best to celebrate or acknowledge these occasions. You might just want to skip them completely. How soon these holidays fall after the death will also play a role in how you feel about participating in them.

Like all other firsts it's important to *do* something to acknowledge these special events. As far as the holidays are concerned that might mean doing the same thing you've always done, or it may mean doing things a little differently this year. The key is to *do something* even if you don't feel like it. This relates to the concept discussed in Chapter 5: *just do it* – don't wait for feelings to be your signal to act. Unfortunately, doing nothing won't take away your pain and can often make things worse as you're left with more time to sit and think about the death of your loved one.

When you are approaching a first it is important to do something to acknowledge the special date.

Many people report that they feel as though they are getting worse in the lead-up to the holidays, especially because these occasions are so commercially driven that they're promoted months before the actual day. It's hard to go about your everyday business without seeing something in the shops or magazines that reminds you of the holiday. It's likely that you'll experience more intense waves of grief during this time. This is normal and the pattern varies in intensity for everyone. But just knowing to expect it can help you get through it. The following strategies can help you plan for the holidays – each one is explained in more detail below.

- Speak to your family about the holidays
- Consider making changes to your usual plans
- Give yourself permission to feel sad and to cry
- Lower your expectations about holiday preparations

- Look after yourself
- Be patient with yourself
- Remember your loved one
- Give yourself permission to enjoy yourself without feeling guilty
- Challenge your unhelpful thoughts

1. Speak to your family about the holidays

Arrange a time to meet with your family to discuss the holidays. You may find that they have been reluctant to bring up the topic or have been avoiding it for fear of making you feel 'sadder'. Unfortunately it's one of those things that won't go away. You'll feel a greater sense of control by opening up this issue for discussion. Think about what you would like to do over the holidays. Think about what your loved one would want you to do. This might give you a starting point. If there are children in your family it's important to let them continue to share in holiday traditions and festivities.

2. Consider making changes to your usual plans

For the first year, you might find it too difficult to do what you've always done on special occasions. This is a very common response but there are ways to help ease the pain. Try adapting family traditions or create new ones – you might want to consider some of the following changes.

- The location of the family gathering
- The time of the gathering
- The number of people you invite
- The number of greetings cards you send
- The number of presents you buy
- The amount of decorating you do
- The amount of cooking you do

I could not face Christmas at our house the first year after my husband died. He always helped with the cooking and carved the meat. So we had it at my daughter's house with her husband and his family. It helped me to get through the day. The second year we had Christmas at my house again and it was much easier — time had gone on and my pain had eased. It all ended up changing again after my grandchildren were born.

LILLIAN, 62

When our daughter died suddenly at the age of 22, I didn't want to think about Christmas. I wanted to avoid it and just stay in my bed until January. I knew this wouldn't take away my pain, nor would it help the rest of our family who were suffering too. So we all decided to do something different that first year because staying home was too hard. We helped out at a homeless shelter and then went to a restaurant afterwards. It felt good to help others and I know my daughter would have been proud

*of us. I'm not sure what we will do this Christmas but I
am glad it won't be the first.*

DORIS, 53

3. Give yourself permission to feel sad and to cry

As discussed in Chapter 3, it's important to be able to express
your pain and not feel as though you have to put on a brave
front for others. Giving yourself permission to feel sad during the holidays and to cry is a necessary part of overcoming
your grief. It's not a sign that you are getting worse – if
you keep in mind the continuous wave-like pattern of grief
it will help you acknowledge that the holidays are likely
to trigger waves of significant intensity. The build-up of
emotion associated with the memories of past holidays and
family gatherings needs to be released. Many people find it
beneficial to set aside a time to focus on the meaning of the
holidays before the actual day. If you can let go of some of
your emotions beforehand, you'll be tackling the anticipation factor head on. Work through exercise 8.4 before the
holidays arrive.

EXERCISE 8.4: GIVE YOURSELF PERMISSION TO CRY

Plan a time and place where you can be alone with
your grief, to think about your loved one at this
time of year. Try to answer these questions. Don't

---

be afraid to let your emotions out – they are all a normal part of your grief.

1. What are your fondest memories of this time with them?
2. What would you say to them about these holidays?
3. What will you miss about them the most?
4. What would they say to you about your first holidays without them?

4. Lower your expectations about holiday preparations

Any festive holiday period is typically very busy with shopping for presents and preparing menus and meals, not to mention sending holiday cards and carrying on with everyday life. Most people find this time of year particularly tiring and stressful. So when you consider that anyone who is grieving typically is tired, lethargic and unmotivated, preparing for the holidays with this added emotional strain sounds like an onerous task. You need to give yourself permission to do less than usual this year, which means you might have to address your thinking and challenge any unrealistic expectations. Be realistic about what you can do. If you feel like things are too much, you need to find ways to cut back on what you think needs to be done. You might also need to delegate or ask for help. Exercise 8.5 will help you manage your holiday preparations.

I decided that this year I couldn't send my usual cards for Chanukah because I'd only just finished writing thank you notes for the sympathy cards. I know my friends and family will understand.

JULIA, 55

EXERCISE 8.5: LOWER YOUR EXPECTATIONS ABOUT HOLIDAY PREPARATIONS

This exercise will help you prioritise your tasks, making it easier to manage the busy holiday season.

Step 1.   List the tasks that need to be done in preparation for the holidays.

Step 2.   Cross out anything you think can be left out this year.

Step 3.   What tasks can you delegate to other family members or friends?

Step 4.   Rank the remaining tasks in order of priority.

Step 5.   Incorporate these tasks into your daily to do list as outlined in Chapter 4.

Step 6.   Lower your expectations. Tell yourself, *It is okay to do less this year.*

5. Look after yourself

Given the holidays are typically a busy time of year for parties and social events, you may receive many invitations to different functions. You need to decide what you can manage and what you can't. You might have to say 'no' and be assertive about your needs even though you may find this difficult. In much the same way as you did in exercise 8.5, you need to decide which functions you will attend and which you will decline. A good guideline is to make your decision based on how at ease you feel with the people who invited you. Being with people who can understand or relate to your pain will be easier than being with those who are constantly trying to cheer you up or expect that you should be 'back to normal' by now.

6. Be patient with yourself

Being patient with yourself relates to your expectations about how you think you *should* be. It's highly likely that you'll encounter many firsts during the holiday season, so this period is a perfect opportunity for you to make sure you're patient with yourself. Be mindful of your self-talk and try not to be critical of things you do or can't do. It's unlikely that you will feel as though you're functioning at 100 per cent, but there's no reason to expect you should be when you are grieving.

7. Remember your loved one

Finding a way to remember your loved one, despite their absence, is one of the most important aspects of getting through the holidays. Families do many different things to acknowledge their loved one. Reminiscing is a great way to bring a sense of them into this difficult first holiday period. What did they enjoy about these holidays? What are some of your favourite stories about past holiday gatherings? Usually once one person starts sharing stories, others follow.

You can also remember them in other ways during the holidays – here are some ideas.

- Buy a candle in honour of them that you can light each year
- Buy or make a special Christmas tree ornament or stocking that you can hang each year
- Ask everyone at the gathering to write down on a small card a fond memory they have of your loved one, and place these memories in a special vase or keepsake box. You can make an occasion of it if you pass the vase or box around the table and ask each person to pick a memory and read it to the group. It's also a great way to reminisce together. And you can easily add to the memories throughout the year at different family functions
- Play your loved one's favourite music for the occasion
- Make their favourite dish
- Make a donation to a charity in their memory
- Plan an event in their honour
- Plant a tree in their memory

After my wife died I invited her closest friends and their families for Christmas drinks. She always loved a party so we toasted her with her favourite wine and talked about the good times. It really helped.

RICHARD, 42

SUGGESTION: INVOLVE THE CHILDREN

When someone dies it's helpful for both adults and children to involve the children in creating new traditions. Take them shopping to buy a special ornament or candle in memory of their loved one and let them participate in the decision-making process.

---

8. Give yourself permission to enjoy yourself without feeling guilty

Many people feel a sense of guilt during the festive season because they are with their family, and their loved one is not. There is a bittersweet quality to the holidays. There will be sadness and a noticeable void, but hopefully there will also be times where you can share a moment of happiness and even laugh with those around you. Some people feel guilty if they do feel happy, even if it is only fleeting happiness. They interpret this as being disrespectful to their loved one's memory. It's important to remind yourself that feeling happy doesn't mean you are forgetting your loved one, or that you love them less. Instead, tell yourself that it is perfectly normal – and in fact healthy – to enjoy the occasion even though your loved one has died. Think about what they would want you to do if you're struggling with feelings of guilt – imagine that they are standing next to you. What would they say? How would they advise you?

9. Challenge unhelpful thoughts

In much the same way as thoughts can lead to guilt, unhelpful thoughts can also lead to other unpleasant feelings. For example you may think, *I can't enjoy anything without my loved one*. This will only serve to intensify your feelings of sadness and despair. Being able to challenge these thoughts and replace them with more helpful, realistic ones can ease your pain. You could try thinking, *It's going to be hard but I will try to enjoy myself*. You can also say to yourself, *What would my loved one want me to do?* Answering this question might give you encouragement and some ideas of what to do.

> *If you are unsure about how to tackle a first ask yourself, What would my loved one want me to do?*

Your loved one's birthday

If you haven't yet reached the date that was your loved one's birthday, you might be concerned about getting through the day. What makes the day particularly difficult – especially the first birthday after their death – is that the date was theirs alone and it magnifies the person's absence. Some families say little about the approaching birthday, while others make elaborate plans. Talking about it ahead of time will help – try to decide as a group if you'd like to celebrate your loved one's birthday. Even though their birthday might be extremely hard, it provides another opportunity to bring friends and family together to reminisce and to maintain a connection. But be prepared that whatever you do in the second year may be quite different from the first. Often as time goes by, and people begin to adjust to life without their loved one, the ways in which you maintain the connection change too.

> *My dad's birthday was a month after he died. We were still in shock at the time and needed to be together as a family on the day. We went out for dinner and got through it as best we could. As the years have gone on we all still acknowledge the date, but now we rarely get together because we don't live as close to each other any-more. Maybe we will organise another gathering for when he would have been 70.*
>
> HANNAH, 40

Wedding and relationship anniversaries

If your spouse or partner has died, the first wedding anniversary or other significant relationship anniversary without them might be a difficult day for you. Even though there are similarities to birthdays and festive holidays, what makes an anniversary different is that it was shared by just the two of you. Anniversaries, even if you didn't celebrate them to any large extent, symbolise the commitment you made to each other. Your family may or may not even acknowledge the date unless you remind them because it probably won't be foremost in their mind. If you suspect that others haven't remembered the date and you want them to, it's up to you to tell them what support you'd like.

Use the framework for tackling firsts to plan how you will acknowledge the date. Is there something special you want to do? The following suggestions may give you some ideas.

- Look through photos or videos of your wedding, honeymoon, or any other special event held to celebrate your relationship
- Play 'your' song – any music that was special to you as a couple
- Buy an anniversary card and write what you'd like to say to them
- Visit their grave
- Remind your friends and family
- Go to a favourite restaurant or haunt
- Decide whether you'd like to be alone or with others
- Carve out time to sit with your grief
- Remind yourself that it normal and expected to feel sad. Give yourself permission to feel emotion and to cry

---

EXERCISE 8.6: FACING WEDDING AND RELATIONSHIP ANNIVERSARIES

If your wedding anniversary or relationship anniversary is approaching, whether or not it is the first one since the death of your loved one, use the framework for tackling firsts to plan how you want to acknowledge the date.

The firsts that never came

For many people who are grieving, there will be significant events they expected to share with their loved one but which never came. If you are grieving the death of a baby you might never have had the first Christmas, Chanukah or other significant occasion or family event. Similarly, with the death of a child there won't be the high school or university graduations, weddings, grandchildren, or other hopes you may have held for their future. Unfortunately parents in these situations often suffer in silence and isolation. As the years go on few people remember or feel comfortable enough to acknowledge these other losses associated with the death of a baby or child. If you are grieving such a death, creating some kind of personal ritual around specific events will help you acknowledge your loved one. For example, lighting a special candle on significant dates or hanging a decoration for them each Christmas will help keep their memory alive, especially if they only touched your life briefly.

Creating a personal ritual around specific events will help you acknowledge your loved one, especially if they only touched your life briefly.

Other firsts that you might now never have the opportunity to experience with your loved one include retirement, being grandparents for the first time, travelling, and moving into a new home. Finding ways to acknowledge these losses is a necessary part of overcoming your grief.

My husband died three months before my retirement. We had decided what we wanted to do over the next twelve months and had made plans to travel and to build a smaller home. We were excited at the prospect of finally being able to do the things we had worked hard for all our lives. I ended up building the house, which was a bittersweet process. It gave me something nice to do and I love it, but when I moved in I felt so sad because he wasn't there to share it with me. I have to keep reminding myself that he would have really loved it too.

ELEANOR, 61

When these events occur think about the four components of the general framework for tackling firsts: anticipation, planning, realistic expectations and reminiscing. It's important to nurture yourself as each event gets closer and closer.

Think about what your loved one would say to you about what you're doing. Imagine what they would be like now. If you are parents of a child who died it might help to build connections with other children who are the same age as your child would have been.

> *When my daughter died at the age of three I continued to remain close to another friend whose daughter was the same age. I made a special effort to remember the little girl's birthday and visit them when I could. It helped me imagine more vividly how my own daughter might have been had she lived. I don't think I will ever stop wondering what she would be like now, but it no longer consumes me like it did in the first few years.*
>
> BRONWYN, 44

> *My mother died from brain cancer about nine months before my wedding. As the day drew near, I decided to see a grief counsellor as I wasn't sure how I would get through the day. She encouraged me to make a plan, which included going to the church alone on the morning of my wedding day to sit quietly and talk to Mum so that when I walked down the aisle I wouldn't be as overcome with emotion. I also asked the minister to speak about Mum briefly and acknowledge her absence during the ceremony. He also lit a candle in her honour. Even though the day at times was hard, preparing in this way helped me feel as though I had a little more control.*
>
> ARDEN, 31

Unexpected firsts

As well as the firsts you're expecting, there will be many that you don't see coming. You might feel as though you have been hit from out of the blue yet again. The actual trigger won't always be obvious, but you can usually identify it with some delving and thought. Unexpected firsts can include a number of things – from seeing someone unexpectedly to realising something of significance, such as the fact you are now an orphan.

My mother died suddenly when I was 18. It was a horrible time in my life but my dad was very supportive and did the best he could. He died nine years later after a short battle with cancer. I had been so busy caring for him in the final weeks that it wasn't until about a month after his death when it really hit me that both my parents were dead. I was an orphan at 27. I felt cheated, especially when I thought that neither of them would be there to see me get married and have children.

Rebecca, 28

SUGGESTION: ORPHANED ADULTS

Interestingly there isn't a word in the English language to describe an adult, especially a young adult, whose parents have both died. We use the word 'orphan' to refer to a child bereaved of both parents.

If you are orphaned as an adult it is important not to minimise the psychological impact of losing both parents, especially as the concept isn't really recognised or discussed. How you view yourself and your world changes and, as with anything to do with grief, you need to give yourself time to adjust to this change.

Coping with unexpected firsts

Even though it is impossible to predict all the firsts, you can use some of the same strategies to cope with the feelings you experience after the event has happened. One of the first signs that you're dealing with something – even if you don't know what it is – will be your mood. In many cases you will realise what triggered your reaction immediately after the event.

When my daughter was three, I was pregnant and had a stillbirth. Even though I was devastated I had to keep going through the motions because I had my daughter to think about. I was able to put on a brave front to some extent, and my family and friends were great – they tried to support me as best they could. But nothing could have prepared me for the day I popped in to my corner shop to buy some milk and the owners asked me whether I'd had a boy or a girl. When I told them that the baby,

*another girl, had died, they were so upset that they had
upset me. I felt devastated again because I thought I was
doing better.*

SALLY, 31

What is the best way, then, to cope with an intense emotional reaction when you're caught off guard? The best
strategy is to begin by examining your thinking just as you
did in Chapter 4. Use the thought diary format to identify
and challenge any unhelpful thoughts. Exercise 8.7 will
help you restructure your thinking to produce more helpful
thoughts that allow you to get through these difficult situations more easily.

EXERCISE 8.7: COPING WITH UNEXPECTED FIRSTS

Step 1. Find a quiet place where you can be alone.

Step 2. Think about the event that just took place.

Step 3. In your journal, use the thought diary
format for the first event you encountered
unexpectedly. You will find a blank thought
diary form in Appendix 2.

A	B	C	D	E
Situation or trigger	Unhelpful thoughts	Feelings (score/10) Behaviour	Helpful thoughts	New feelings (score/10) New behaviour

Step 4. Record in (A) the situation or event you experienced.

What happened? Where were you?

Step 5. In (B), write down your thoughts about (A). Identify any unhelpful thoughts.

Step 6. Next, in (C), list your feelings and behaviour. You can rate the strength of your feelings or emotions from 0–10, with 10 being the strongest.

Step 7. Now, in (D), generate new thoughts that are helpful and realistic. Ask yourself these questions:

1. Where's the evidence for what I thought in (B)?
2. What are the alternatives to what I thought in (B)?
3. What is the likely effect on me of thinking in this way?

4. How would I advise a friend to think in the same situation?

5. What would my loved one tell me if they were here now?

Step 8. If you were to think in the way you described in step 7, what would be your new feelings and behaviour? Write these in (E). Can you make a plan?

Step 9. Remember to stay with your grief and work through your thinking. You might want to avoid thinking about it, but if you do that it will only be harder the next time you're faced with the same or a similar issue.

Here's how Sally completed her thought diary after the upsetting visit to the shop.

SALLY'S DIARY ENTRY

A	B	C	D	E
Situation or trigger	Unhelpful thoughts	Feelings (score/10) Behaviour	Helpful thoughts	New feelings (score/10) New behaviour
Shop owners asking about the baby	*They don't know. I will have to tell them. It's never going to get easier.*	Sadness (9/10) Anxiety (9/10) Crying, left the shop as fast as I could	*Not everyone knows, especially people who aren't close to me. It will get easier as more people know.*	Sadness (9/10) Anxiety (5/10) Plan to visit the shop next week

Being able to identify the triggers and what you thought about them will help you feel more in control and able to make plans for how you tackle other firsts. In Sally's case she was able to reduce her anxiety by challenging her thoughts. Even though she still felt as sad and longed to hold her baby, challenging her thoughts in this way allowed her to work out what she might do next. She decided to visit the shop the following week because she realised that the longer she avoided it, the harder it would become. Even though her sadness and pain were very real, she felt a greater sense of control once she made a plan.

Next steps

The more firsts you have faced, whether or not you had anticipated them, the more you are adjusting to your life without the person who died. It might not feel that way but change is slow. And patience is a must when new learning is involved. There is no way round grief – you need to tackle it head on. Small steps eventually add up to bigger ones.

Chapter 3 introduced the concept of being forced on to a different path, not of your choosing, after the death of someone significant in your life. Part of the struggle of grief is working out how to let go of your old path at the same time as beginning to build a new one. The next chapter will look at how you can build your new path so you can begin to live your life again in a meaningful way, with a sense of purpose.

Summary

- There will be many firsts to face in the year following the death of your loved one – you can't avoid these firsts; working through them is part of grieving
- These firsts often correlate with trigger waves on your overall wave-like pattern of grief

- The framework for tackling firsts includes four important components: anticipation, planning, having realistic expectations and reminiscing
- Be patient with yourself. Getting through each first is part of adjusting to your life now

9

Your new path

Did you ever play the game 'Tug-of-war' when you were a child? Children were divided into two teams and each side took hold of different ends of a long piece of rope. The object of the game was to see which team could pull the other side over a line drawn on the ground marking the middle of the length of rope. If the teams were evenly matched the tugging could go on for some time. Eventually one side would get the better of the other and the losing team would fall over in a heap. This game is very much like the struggle people experience when their loved one dies, as they try to let go of life as they knew it and begin to live a different life. It's a struggle that goes back and forth, many times over. On one hand you know that you need actively to build a new life for yourself, but on the other you don't want to because that means letting go of the life you had before. In time what hopefully happens is that the 'winner' in the tug-of-war game is the decision to build a new life. One important component of making this decision is realising that this doesn't mean forgetting your loved one or 'getting over' their death, but instead finding a way to incorporate your experiences and memories of them into your life as it is now. This chapter will show you how.

The other side of grief

You are forever changed when a significant person in your life dies. Remember the wound analogy from Chapter 3? The death of a loved one leaves a scar that will always be with you and can easily remind you of your loss. But this scar shouldn't prevent you from living your life again. In fact it would be a very depressing world if there was no hope of being happy again after the death of a loved one. The reality is that people do find ways to adapt and move on, and somehow reconcile the death of their loved one.

Hope

What does it mean to have hope about something? *Hope* is defined as 'an emotion characterised by the expectation that one will have positive experiences (or that a potentially threatening or negative situation will not materialise or will ultimately result in a favourable state of affairs); and by the belief that one can influence one's experiences in a positive way'. When you are grieving the death of your loved one and trying to imagine a new life for yourself, it's important to have hope for your future. You hope that eventually your pain will ease; that you will find a renewed sense of purpose in your life; and that one day you will again find some kind of happiness.

Even though many people doubt early on that these things are possible, knowing that others have gone on to find happiness again can form the basis of your hope. Being able to tell yourself that these things are possible is a start. Your thoughts and expectations play an important role in building your new path. Chapter 4 described how thoughts influence feelings and behaviour. In the same way, your thinking is a very important factor in creating hope for a life filled with a sense of purpose once more. What you say to yourself can be the deciding factor. You want your thoughts to bring about a sense of hope for your future. Being able to tell yourself the following things might help you do this.

- It is possible to find meaning again in my life
- Other people have gone on to enjoy their life again and so can I
- I will need to work hard at creating this new life but I can do it
- It will take time but it is possible to be happy again in a different way
- ___ would want me to go on and be happy
- ___ would not want me to dwell on the past forever
- ___ would want me to make the best of my life
- Living a new life doesn't mean forgetting my old one

It is important to have hope for your future: to hope that eventually your pain will ease; that you will find a renewed sense of purpose; and that one day you will again find some kind of happiness.

What do you hope your life will look like on the other side of your grief? This is a good question to ask yourself. It may be a difficult one to answer right now, but it will start you thinking about shaping your future. Perhaps there are things you want to change and maybe you've learnt lessons from your loved one that will influence the direction you take.

What do I want my life to look like? I want to be the best dad I can for my three young children. Before my wife died I worked long hours and often didn't see them through the week. Now they only have me so I want to be there with them, bringing them up in the way we always planned. I want to be much more involved in their lives.

TOBY, 43

Olivia was able to articulate her hopes for the future in the same way, even though her husband had died only recently.

I know I am a long way from this but I can see a life for myself on the other side of my grief. It has something to do with living near the ocean where I can spend my days writing. I've always enjoyed writing children's stories, but had to put this on hold while I cared for my husband.

When I write I feel a wonderful sense of achievement, which I know helps me.

OLIVIA, 52

Now complete exercise 9.1 to start exploring your new life.

EXERCISE 9.1 THE OTHER SIDE OF YOUR GRIEF

What do you hope your life will look like on the other side of your grief? Jot down any ideas, even if you don't consider them to be possibilities at the moment.

Deciding to move forward

Before you can get to the other side of your grief, you actually need to decide that this is what you want to do. It might seem like a 'choice-less choice' but it's important to have a conversation with yourself about why it's necessary to move forward and what it means to you. You could find yourself at a crossroads where you know deep down that you need to make this decision, but you're not quite sure how to do it. It is crucial to understand that 'moving forward' does not require you to forget your loved one and the life you shared. Rather, it means finding ways to live your life again with a sense of purpose. Working out what it is that will give you this sense of purpose will take some trial and error, and might not be immediately obvious.

Moving forward with your life does not mean forgetting your loved one or the life you shared.

If you look back to Chapter 1 you'll see again that, although grieving is painful, it's also good because it gives you the time and space to work out what you need to do to *adjust* to life without your loved one. So it makes sense that, if the main focus is adjusting to change, the greater the change in your life following the death, the greater the adjustment you'll need to make. This in turn affects how different your new path will be. Remember that adjusting to change means adjusting to changes at an emotional, physical and cognitive level.

What if I'm stuck?

If you are having difficulty getting to the point of being able to say to yourself, *I need to move forward,* or, *I'm ready to move forward,* it might be useful to look at your thinking. Often thoughts can keep you stuck, as though you are a car with spinning wheels. The way to get yourself 'unstuck' is to identify these unhelpful thoughts and challenge them, much like you did in Chapter 4. Here are some of the thoughts that typically keep people stuck.

- My life is over
- This is not how it was meant to be
- Life isn't fair
- What's happened to me isn't fair
- There's nothing worth living for now
- Nothing will ever be the same again
- If I build a new life I might forget the old one
- I'll feel guilty if I go on with my life because I will think I'm being disloyal to my loved one

These unhelpful thoughts tend to fall into one of four categories.

1. Life isn't fair
2. Life is over
3. Fear about forgetting your loved one
4. Feelings of guilt about continuing on

Thoughts like these are considered unhelpful and self-defeating because they are likely to prevent you from moving forward. If you don't challenge and restructure these types of thoughts, the possible consequences of continuing to think in this way include withdrawing from others, becoming clinically depressed and, in extreme cases, thoughts or acts of suicide.

If you feel you're stuck, use the technique of asking questions to challenge unhelpful thoughts – exercise 9.2 will show you how. Remember that challenging your thoughts won't be easy at first. Just like any new skill it takes lots of practice before it becomes second nature.

EXERCISE 9.2: CHALLENGING THE THOUGHTS THAT ARE KEEPING YOU STUCK

Use your journal to complete this exercise.

Step 1. Spend five minutes thinking about moving forward on a new path. What thoughts come to mind about achieving this? Write them down.

Step 2. Which of the four categories listed above do your thoughts fall into (unfair, life is over, fear of forgetting, feelings of guilt)?

Step 3. Ask yourself the following questions:

1. How would I advise a friend to think in the same situation?
2. What would my loved one tell me to do if they were here now?
3. How can I think differently so that I begin to build my life without my loved one?

Step 4. Now think again about moving forward on a new path.

Write down your thoughts, as you did in step 1.

Linda used this exercise after her 56-year-old husband was killed in a car accident. They had been married for twenty-nine years and their three children had left home to go to university. With the children gone, Linda and her husband were planning their first overseas holiday. She described their marriage as 'distant' – her hope had been that the trip would be the turning point for them so they could get their relationship back on track. Linda was devastated when her husband died. All she could think of was that life wasn't fair because they had been robbed of the chance to rebuild their relationship.

Linda came for counselling six months after her husband's death. She believed that there was nothing left for her now – that her life was over at the age of 51. She loved her children but felt that they had their own lives now. She was stuck and didn't know what she could do to move forward.

CHALLENGING THE THOUGHTS THAT ARE KEEPING YOU STUCK: LINDA'S ANSWERS

Step 1. Spend five minutes thinking about moving forward on a new path. What thoughts come to mind about achieving this? Write them down. *I feel as though my life is over. It is so unfair that my husband was killed when it was our chance to be together to try to salvage our marriage.*

Step 2. Which of the four categories listed above do your thoughts fall into (unfair, life is over, fear of forgetting, feelings of guilt)? *Life is unfair and my life is over.*

Step 3. Ask yourself the following questions.

1. How would I advise a friend in the same situation? *That there are never any guarantees in life – life isn't fair. Your life has changed – it has not turned out in the way you wanted it to, but that doesn't mean it's over.*

2. What would my loved one tell me to do if they were here now? *He would tell me that I need to find things in my life that bring me enjoyment, that I have to get on with things, and that I still need to be involved with the kids.*

3. How can I think differently so that I begin to build my life without my loved one? *I have a choice to make. I can either continue to tell myself that my life is over or I can tell myself my life has changed – that I need to work hard to find new things that are important to me and which bring meaning to my life.*

Step 4. Now think again about moving forward on a new path. Write down your thoughts as you did in step 1. *My life isn't over – I'm only 51 and I've got many years ahead of me. My life with my husband has ended and that isn't fair, but then many things in life aren't fair. We both knew that we were going to work on rebuilding our marriage and I am thankful for that.*

Over the course of several months Linda worked hard at challenging her unhelpful thoughts. She returned to work and joined a support group for widows and widowers. She also became involved in her local political organisation – something in which she had always been interested but hadn't had the time for when her children were young. Slowly, Linda is building a new life for herself with purpose and a renewed sense of meaning. She is trying to let go of her belief that her life is over.

WARNING! PROFESSIONAL HELP NEEDED

If you have been working your way through the different exercises in *Overcoming Grief* and feel as though nothing is helping you, or you believe you are getting worse, then now is the time to seek professional help. If you are having difficulty challenging your thoughts, you feel hopeless about your future, or you are thinking about suicide, then put this book down. Contact your nearest health care agency, doctor or friend immediately, who can help you get the support you need.

Look back to 'A note of caution' at the beginning of the book, to the list of warning signs that need to be taken seriously. Seek help from a doctor, grief counsellor or clinical psychologist if you experience any of these symptoms consistently, for more than a week or two, and if you feel as though you are getting worse.

Building your new path

Once you have made the decision to work actively on building your new path, you need to make sure your expectations are realistic about how easily and quickly this will happen. You need to expect that you could have many false starts, that it might be very bumpy at times, and that your new path will take time to evolve. If you think this way you won't be shocked or disappointed when things don't go as smoothly as you thought they would.

Make sure your expectations are realistic. Expect to have false starts as you find your way on your new path.

Chapter 3 explained how the death of your loved one forced you on to a different path not of your choosing. This path is unknown and unfamiliar, and not where you want to be. Figure 9.1 illustrates this forced change.

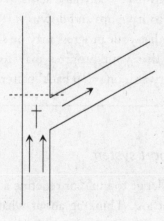

Figure 9.1 A different path

Death inevitably brings change, so it is reasonable to expect that the greatest amount of change and adjustment will probably occur in the first part of this new path. At this time, immediately after your loved one's death, everything is different. It's important to understand that you are likely to encounter lots of ups and downs as you travel along this new path, in much the same way as your grief follows a wave-like pattern with good and bad days, and trigger waves that often come out of the blue. In time this new path will become familiar and feel quite normal as you get used to doing things differently.

TIPS FOR KEEPING YOUR EXPECTATIONS REALISTIC ABOUT BUILDING YOUR NEW PATH

- Expect to have many false starts
- Expect to have ups and downs
- Expect that your progress may be slow
- Expect that your progress may follow a 'two steps forward, one step back' pattern

Create a support system

It is a huge challenge to build or redefine a new life following a significant loss. Thinking about what this entails too soon after a loved one's death can be overwhelming. For this reason health professionals encourage people who are grieving to take it one day at a time in the beginning, and to avoid making major and potentially irreversible decisions too soon after a death.

When you find yourself at the point where you believe that you have enough energy to begin to focus on building your new path, it's vital to ensure that you have a solid support system around you. You possibly already have good support from those who have been there for you since the death. You might also find that your needs change as time goes on, and that you need other types of support in addition to this core group. Some people find that they now need to be around others who can encourage them to try different things and who are comfortable with them taking this approach. It's important to surround yourself with people whose company you enjoy, who you believe have your best interests at heart, and with whom you feel at ease. If some of your 'supporters' are critical and negative about what you're doing or not doing, consider whether they're really providing the support you need. If you don't have the support of friends or family, or if their support is no longer constructive, you will need to find it in other places such as bereavement groups, self-help materials or by seeing a grief counsellor.

TIPS FOR CREATING A SUPPORT SYSTEM

- Associate with friends and family with whom you are comfortable
- Read self-help books or watch self-help DVDs
- Join a bereavement support group – either locally or online
- See a grief counsellor or a health professional who is experienced in working with people who have been bereaved
- Attend a church or religious group
- Join a group that is specific to your loss – for example a group for widows/widowers, suicide survivors, parents who have lost children, or a Sudden Infant Death support group

---

I was a mess after my daughter died. I felt as though I was in a fog that I couldn't find my way out of. I had to keep going for my other children but every day was a struggle. I started seeing a grief counsellor where I spent a lot of time in the first few months talking about my daughter, crying my heart out and trying to imagine life without her. This was the only place I felt safe to let myself go – at home I felt that I needed to be strong for my husband and kids. I felt some relief after the first anniversary of her death because I knew I had survived the first year – just. I also knew that I had to do something different – I couldn't stay the way I was. With the help of my counsellor I worked on redefining my life without my daughter. I joined a group for parents whose children had died and found great comfort from being with other people who knew something of my pain. I also decided to go back to work three days a week, which gave me a new focus. Slowly life is getting a little easier and now her memory spurs me on – I can hear her saying 'keep going, Mum'.

AMANDA, 46

It's important to surround yourself with people whose company you enjoy and who you believe have your best interests at heart.

Seek opportunities to try new things

Most people find that their different path involves new things as well as some of the same things that were a part of their old life. You might actively pursue new interests while others evolve over time. Try to keep in mind these general guidelines.

- Be open to trying new things
- Seek opportunities to try new things
- When you attempt something for the first time, try it at least twice before you dismiss it as a possibility
- Be mindful of your self-talk. Tell yourself, *Anything new will feel strange at first*
- Start with whatever's easiest and build up to the harder things
- Ask a friend to go with you if you feel a little nervous
- Sometimes, be spontaneous
- Try things that are inexpensive so cost isn't the factor that prevents you from continuing

---

If you are not sure where to start, exercise 9.3 can give you some ideas about how to find purpose and meaning again.

EXERCISE 9.3: SEEK OPPORTUNITIES TO TRY NEW THINGS

1. What types of activities have you enjoyed in the past?

   - Sports
   - Hobbies
   - Interest groups
   - Volunteer organisations
   - Church/faith-based groups
   - Community groups

2. What activities have you always wanted to try and never had the opportunity?
3. What organisations are you interested in?
4. What are or were you passionate about in your life?

After my wife died I started volunteering one day a week for Meals on Wheels. It helped me a lot — it got me out of the house and it felt good to be able to do something to help those in need.

HARRY, 63

I'd always wanted to travel overseas but my husband had never really wanted to, so I never pushed it. I also felt we had other priorities when he was alive. About six months after his death my son had to travel to Europe for business and asked me to go with him. I loved every moment of it and now I'm planning my next trip with an over-55s tour group.

ALISON, 65

What would your loved one want for you?

If you are struggling with building your new path, many people find it helpful to think about what their loved one would want for them. Most people say they would want them to be happy, but by using exercise 9.4 you can try to take it a step further.

EXERCISE 9.4: WHAT WOULD YOUR LOVED ONE WANT FOR YOU?

Imagine your loved one is sitting next to you now. Think about what suggestions they would offer. What things did they know you enjoyed? What things did you enjoy together? What did your plans entail? Now try answering these questions.

1. What would your loved one want for you now?
2. Did you ever talk about life without each other? What did your loved one say?
3. What plans did you have together? Which ones could you do on your own or with someone else?

---

4. What advice would your loved one give you about moving forward without them?

5. If your roles were reversed, what suggestions would you offer them?

My husband and I were about to start our retirement when he died. Our plans for our future together were shattered in a moment and the direction I thought my life was taking took a dramatic turn. Everything I had hoped for was gone, never to be possible again. Now, many years later, I have rebuilt my life with the help of my family and friends. I've never remarried or wanted to, but I have found a certain level of contentment. I've been able to do some of the things that I had expected to do with my husband. I've travelled, enjoyed my grandchildren and built a retirement home. I've pursued other interests too that maybe I wouldn't have considered had he still been alive. Even though I wish it hadn't turned out this way, I can say that my life is good and I am happy.

MARGO, 71

A glimpse of my old self

Chapter 5 introduced the idea of *just doing it* rather than waiting to *feel* like doing something. By going through the motions and developing a routine, the hope is that this helps you to get through the day more easily. The same advice also applies to building your new path. At times you might become despondent because it seems harder than you thought. But by trying to do things that you know you enjoy, or which you have enjoyed in the past, you will increase your chances of building a new and meaningful path. Many people who have been bereaved talk about the first time they actually felt like their old self again. This feeling might be fleeting and it may take you a while to realise its significance, but this moment and similar moments that follow can give you hope that it is possible to return to something of your former self. Like every aspect of grief, this will happen for people at different times.

> *It was about seven months after my husband died when, for the first time, I saw a glimpse of my old self. I'd invited some friends over, and as I was preparing the meal I actually found myself enjoying what I was doing. It was a significant moment for me as it gave me hope that I could get through this and come out the other side.*
>
> CHARLOTTE, 57

Make it the best it can be

Once you start trying new things and gain a sense of the direction in which you are heading, you may want to think about setting goals for the things you would like to achieve in the next few months. Make sure that any goals you set yourself are realistic and also flexible in case your circumstances change. It's a good idea to think first about what you would like to achieve in the next six months. Then towards the end of that time, plan goals for the following six months. Exercise 9.5 will help you think about your goals.

EXERCISE 9.5 SETTING FUTURE GOALS

Step 1. What would you like to achieve in the next six months? Be specific – describe the goal as fully as possible and consider the following areas:

- Leisure activities/hobbies
- Health and fitness
- Financial planning
- Travel
- Career/education
- Community service/volunteering
- Extended family
- Children
- Grandchildren
- Friendships

Step 2. What action do you need to take to achieve your goals?

Step 3. As you achieve your goals, continue to set new ones.

Re-examine your identity

After the rawness of your grief lessens a little and the majority of the administrative tasks have been completed, you may find yourself thinking more about your identity and how it has been impacted by the death of your loved one. This is especially relevant if your partner or your child has died, as your identity is closely linked to the roles you have in life. The best advice is to carve out time to think carefully about re-examining your identity and what it means to you. It's a process that evolves over time and requires working out what's important to you.

> *After my son died, I struggled with knowing how to respond when somebody asks me 'How many children do you have?' I had always seen myself as a mother to a son and to a daughter. It helped me to think about who I was and the response that I wanted to give. I decided that I would answer this question by saying, 'I have two children, Megan is 7 and Charlie would have been 5, but he died in January.'*
>
> ADRIANA, 35

A new direction

As time goes on, many people who have been bereaved are able to say they feel as though they have reconciled or grieved the death of their loved one, even though they will never forget them. Statements like these probably mean different things to different people, but they probably have something to do with an acceptance that life is now different. Some people continue in their lives in much the same way as before, while others go on to have new relationships or more children.

Loving again

It *is* possible to love again when someone you love dies. Some people remarry or have other significant relationships, they may have another child, and many develop other meaningful friendships. Forming new relationships often produces many mixed emotions both for the person who has been bereaved as well as for other family members. There can be happiness and sadness, excitement and fear, not to mention guilt. Many people fail to understand that, even if you go on to have another relationship or another child, it is absolutely possible to find a special place in your heart and mind to remember the person who died. These relationships aren't mutually exclusive and love is not finite. Loving again doesn't mean you didn't love in the first place. Finding love in a different place, at a different time in your life, does not negate the love you had for the person who died. Loving again doesn't mean you've forgotten your loved one.

Love is not mutually exclusive. Loving again doesn't mean you didn't love in the first place or that you have forgotten your loved one who died.

TACKLING GUILT

Guilt is often a huge issue in new relationships that are formed after the death of a loved one. If you're in this position and you're feeling a sense of guilt, it's an issue you need to address. Chapter 4 introduced guilt as the emotion you experience when you think you have done something wrong. It's important to identify your thoughts and challenge them so that you can get to the point of being able to say, *I have done nothing wrong by loving someone else.*

> *My wife died three years ago. We had a wonderful marriage that lasted thirty-five years and our two children have been a great support to me since she died. About six months ago I started dating a woman I have known socially for the last few years. She is also widowed and seems happy to spend time with me. My problem is that I feel pangs of guilt when we're together – guilt about being with another woman as well as guilt about enjoying life again. My children are supportive although I think deep down they would prefer it if I was still on my own. I don't want to remarry but I would like to be able to have a close relationship without worrying about whether I am being disloyal to my wife.*
>
> DANIEL, 66

Daniel needed to challenge his thinking otherwise his guilt would have prevented him from enjoying a new relationship. So he used the thought diary format to restructure his thinking, which allowed him to continue his new relationship without feeling guilty. He was also able to tell himself that this new relationship could never take away his memories of his wife, and that it didn't make sense to compare the two relationships as they were totally different. As he continued to challenge his thinking in this way, he felt less guilty and a sense of relief.

DANIEL'S THOUGHT DIARY

A	B	C	D	E
Situation or trigger	Unhelpful thoughts	Feelings (score/10) Behaviour	Helpful thoughts	New feelings (score/10) New behaviour
Starting a new relationship	*I am being disloyal. I feel as though I am being unfaithful.*	Guilt (7/10)	*I have done nothing wrong. My wife would want me to date if I met someone. I would want the same for her if the situation was reversed.*	Relief (7/10)

If you are feeling guilty because of a new relationship, use exercise 9.6 to explore these feelings.

EXERCISE 9.6: TACKLING GUILT IN A NEW RELATIONSHIP

Are you in a new relationship and experiencing feelings of guilt? Use the thought diary framework to challenge your guilty thinking and generate new, helpful thoughts as Daniel did. You can use your journal, or you will find a blank thought diary form in Appendix 2.

AVOID RUSHING IN

Everyone's situation is different, but it is generally advisable not to jump into another relationship too soon after the death of a loved one. The logic behind this advice is that you risk making a decision based on emotion rather than on fact. Sometimes people start new relationships as a way of coping with their pain, but unfortunately this can potentially set them up for even more heartache.

My husband died after a short battle with cancer. Not long after his death I was reintroduced to an old classmate of mine. We hadn't seen each other in twenty-five years, but when we met again there was something comfortable and familiar. Before long I was infatuated and felt the excitement of new love. Unfortunately as the novelty wore off, I realised that this relationship wasn't for me. We ended up breaking up about a year after my husband died. Then I found myself back in the depths of my grief and it seemed worse this time because now I was really alone.

DEIDRE, 49

Continue on your new path

In Chapter 1 you began to tell your story – your story about your loved one and the effect their death has had on your life. When someone you love dies, your life story changes. It doesn't continue in the way you had expected or hoped. Maybe up until that point you hadn't really considered your life story and the events that would shape who you are. But their death has forced upon you an awareness of your life story and the new path your life must now take.

It was a Monday – September 9 – a day I will never forget. I think I can track just about every minute of that day. My organisation had sent me on a five-day conference, which I'd really been looking forward to. It was a beautiful, sunny day. The speaker for the afternoon session had just begun when he was interrupted with an urgent message for someone. At that instant I knew my name was going to be called out. Little did I know that from then on my life would change forever. As I left the room my initial thought was that there must be a crisis at work. I never imagined the call would be my brother-in-law telling me that my father had had a car accident and was in a hospital an hour's drive away. He didn't know whether he was dead or alive, or if he did, he didn't say. I drove as fast as I could, hoping and praying that he would be alive, sitting up in his hospital bed full of cheek. Instead I was met by my sister who told me that our father was dead. Dead at 56. Instead of seeing him in the hospital bed I saw him in the morgue. How did that happen? Now, sixteen years on, I can recall these events without raw or intense emotion. The sadness is still there at a deep level, especially if I think about the 'what could have beens', but life has gone on, which is what my dad would have wanted. He was the father that most people wished for. I was lucky to have him. Not only did he teach me about life, but he also taught me about death and how to go on living.

SUE, 43

If you have worked your way through *Overcoming Grief* you might still feel that you have a long way to go. That's perfectly normal. Your challenge now is to continue to work on making your new path the most rewarding it can be, even though you wish things were the way they used to be. You might find it helpful from time to time to review the strategies and exercises outlined in *Overcoming Grief* – they will help you in different ways at different times. The final chapter of this book is written specifically for people who are supporting someone who is grieving, so you may want to show it to the people who care about you. Wherever you find yourself now, hopefully you will have begun to feel that the hold grief has on you is lessening. And soon, if not now, you will catch the first glimpse of what your life might look like on the other side of your grief.

Summary

- It's important to have hope when you build your new path
- Moving forward does not mean forgetting your loved one
- Challenge the thoughts that keep you stuck
- Set goals and seek opportunities to try new things
- If ever you are stuck, or you are having unhelpful thoughts, ask yourself, *What would my loved one want for me?*

For those who care

Many people find that talking about death feels awkward and they prefer to avoid the subject whenever possible. Others can't really relate and end up saying the wrong thing. But when someone you care about is grieving, your support is invaluable during this difficult time. Even though you can never know another person's pain, it's a good start simply to have an understanding of grief and an idea of how to help. This chapter is written specifically for people who care about someone who is grieving – whether that person is a friend, relative or colleague. It gives a brief overview of grief and offers a number of practical suggestions about how to provide support. The chapter also outlines ideas for initiating discussions with loved ones about grief and about preparing for death. As a society, the more we talk about death and accept it as a part of everyday life, the easier it will become for those who are grieving the death of a loved one.

Grief at a glance

Grief can best be described as the intense emotional and physical reaction that someone experiences following the death of a loved one. People can also experience grief responses in relation to other losses such as divorce and retirement. In psychological terms *grief* is defined as 'the anguish experienced after significant loss, usually the death of a beloved person'. People report a number of common reactions after someone significant in their life dies (see table 2.1 in Chapter 2). Usually the physical reactions ease sooner than the emotional ones, which can go on for months or even years, often unnoticed by those around.

Grief is unique

No two people will experience the death of a loved one in the same way. How someone expresses their pain depends on a number of factors. It varies according to their personality, the way they cope with problems, the way they view the world, the circumstances surrounding the death, their support system, and their experience with death in general. Even if they have experienced the death of other people who were close to them, each loss can affect them in different ways. There is no single or right way to grieve, so it's unhelpful to make comparisons about grief. If you are supporting someone who is grieving, remember that it doesn't help to hear that someone else's loss is 'worse' because this won't help ease the pain. It also does not help to tell them that you know how they are feeling because this is impossible – you cannot truly know their pain or sense of loss.

It's also important to be aware of your own feelings about death and dying when you are providing this support. Death affects everyone at some stage, unlike other problems that only some people ever experience such as anxiety disorders or depression. When you see another person's pain it is not uncommon to think, *This could be me*. Exercise 10.1 will help you think more about your own experiences of death and dying.

EXERCISE 10.1: YOUR OWN EXPERIENCES OF DEATH AND GRIEF

Spend some time thinking about each question, then note down what comes to mind.

1. What experiences have you had of death and grief?
2. Was there anything that really helped you as you grieved?
3. Were there things that people did or didn't do that were unhelpful or even upsetting at the time?

Loss and change

From a psychological perspective, loss and change are two of the major components of grief. When someone close to you dies you lose not only the person, but also all the other things they represented. So someone who is grieving a loved one's death may also be grieving the loss of their mentor, companion, provider, nurturer, financial advisor, sounding board and their hopes for the future. If you think about how many losses a person has to face, it's easy to see why grief cannot be over in an instant and why it takes time and effort to deal with all these losses.

> *When my husband died last year my life was turned upside down. We were both due to retire at the end of the year and we were planning a trip to Hong Kong and Australia. I feel so cheated that I have lost not only my husband, but also our chance really to enjoy our retirement together.*
>
> ELAINE, 58

When a loved one dies, the person who has been bereaved has to face many losses, not just the loss of the person.

Change is an inevitable result of the many losses that occur after the death of a loved one. How much change someone has to endure correlates with how much their lives overlapped, both physically and emotionally. Consider, for example, a couple who have been married for fifty years or more and depend greatly on each other. When one of them dies the change and associated adjustment for the other can be significant. The one who has been bereaved may have to move house or take on roles they never had in their life before. So it's easy to see why statements such as 'at least they had a good life', which are often made in an attempt to ease somebody's pain, don't help at all if you're supporting someone to adjust to life without their loved one. In fact statements like these can often make matters worse because they send a signal that someone shouldn't be feeling sorry for themself – that they were 'lucky' to have their loved one in their life for as long as they did. Once someone senses that others think this way, they are more likely to avoid conversations about how they are feeling.

Even if you have experienced the death of a loved one, it is important not to assume that the person you are now supporting will have the same experience as you. Although your experience might give you a sense of what they are going through, you can never truly know their pain. Listening to them is probably the best thing that you can do, especially when their grief is new. Try to resist the urge to tell them what to do even if you believe you have good advice to give. If they ask for your input you can offer your suggestions, but always try to preface your advice with, *What I found helpful was . . .*, rather than, *You should do this . . .*

Resist the urge to tell someone what to do.

If you want to get a sense of what loss and change actually feels like, turn back to exercise 2.2 in Chapter 2 'Writing with your other hand' where the reader was asked to write their name and address with their non-dominant hand. This will give you some idea of why someone who has been bereaved finds it so difficult to function in the first few months following the death of their loved one. They know how to live but something has changed, something is different – there will have to be lots of adjustments before life feels remotely comfortable.

Control

The concept of control is another important psychological component of grief. When somebody's loved one dies, they have little or no control over the circumstances surrounding the death. They can feel overwhelmed by their grief, and often people who have been bereaved report that it feels as though their grief has total control over them. Part of supporting someone as they grieve is to help them regain a sense of control in their life. But being patient with them is a must – it will take them time and lots of trial and error to regain control.

Expectations

From a cognitive point of view, an expectation is a mindset about how we think something *will* be. If you think about it you probably have expectations about a number of things in your life, even though these expectations often go unnoticed. You might have expectations about your relationships, your work and your performance in different situations. You might also have expectations about how others should be when they are grieving the loss of a loved one. You may find it difficult to provide support if someone is grieving in a way that's different to your expectation of how they should grieve.

Today we live in a very fast-paced and technology-driven world that perpetuates a 'fix it', 'can do' mentality. We want things done immediately and we have little patience. We send an email and expect a response in hours; we visit the doctor and expect a prescription to make us feel better; and we can cook a frozen meal in the microwave in a matter of minutes. Unfortunately grief doesn't follow these same rules. It knows no timetable and it cannot be forced or hurried. In fact it seems as though grief has a life of its own. If you can accept that there is no set timetable for grief you'll be less likely to make unhelpful remarks that could be hurtful or upsetting. Later in this chapter we'll look more closely at what not to say to someone who is grieving.

It's no surprise then that people, including those who are grieving, believe that grief should be something they can 'get over quickly' so they can 'return to normal' in much the same way as you'd recover from an infection. The problem is that this view of grief is incorrect. Grief is not an illness – it's a normal and expected response to the death of a loved one. It is a highly individualised process that involves many ups and downs. You might hear it described as a 'two steps forward, one step back' pattern, even though at times it may feel like two steps forward and three steps back.

Grief is not an illness with a prescribed cure.

When a loved one dies, the lives of the people closest to them are changed forever. Part of grieving involves someone working out what their 'new' life without their loved one will look like. The process of grieving gives them the time and space, at both an emotional and a cognitive level, to adjust to life without their loved one. Most people who have experienced the death of someone close to them would say that while they never got over the death, they were able to learn to live without their loved one.

One of the greatest challenges of supporting someone who has been bereaved is accepting that even though we live in a 'fix it' world, there is nothing you can do to fix their problem. Once you accept this fact you'll be more likely to be able to offer the types of support they need. If you're at a loss to know what to say, *ask* what support you can give – simply say, *How can I help you?* It's also important to realise that if you are both grieving the same loss, you might not be able to offer the type of support someone needs. You need to look after your own needs too and be realistic about what you can and can't provide.

The experience of grief

With this 'fix it' mentality, many people expect that somebody's 'progress' through their grief should be linear. In other words they think, *The more time that goes by, the better I will feel* (see figure 10.1). This belief is not only unhelpful, it's also inaccurate.

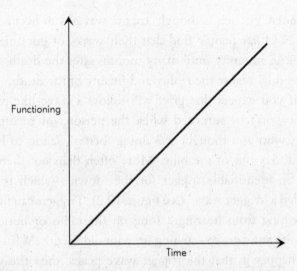

Figure 10.1 Unrealistic expectations about progress

The experience of grief is best described as following a wave-like pattern. People report that their grief tends to come in waves, with these individual waves joined together to form a continuous wave that reflects their experience of grief over time. Some people find the individual waves to be very intense whereas others find that they're not that strong at all. Thinking of grief as coming in waves is a good way to illustrate how everyone will have their own individual experience of grief. No two people will have the same wave-like pattern of grief – there will be different triggers at different times and people will experience waves of varying intensities. Many people report that the waves of grief hit frequently and are very intense soon after the death of a loved one. As time passes their intensity and frequency lessen, although 'trigger waves' can occur at any time. Other people find that their waves of grief may not peak in intensity until many months after the death, when they fully realise the reality and finality of the death.

If you expect that grief will follow a wave-like pattern you won't be surprised when the person you're support-ing, who you thought was doing 'better', seems to have a 'bad' day out of the blue. More often than not there will be an identifiable trigger for the 'down', which is often called a 'trigger wave' (see figure 10.2). Triggers can include anything from hearing a song on the radio or noticing a significant date, to catching up with old friends. What tends to happen is that the trigger wave peaks, then the wave-like pattern continues on. It is important for people who have been bereaved to understand that the intense emotions that accompany trigger waves – which often include a deep yearning for their loved one – do not mean they are getting worse or going crazy. They are simply normal reactions.

The 'stage' theory of grief

Historically, grief has commonly been conceptualised as occurring in different stages, even though there has been little empirical evidence to support this model. It was believed that people who had been bereaved needed to progress through a number of different stages – including denial and anger – in order to grieve properly. Now it is believed that grief is not linear, but rather an individual-ised, complex response to loss. Much of the recent research

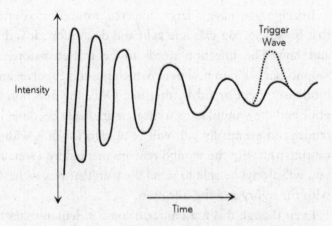

Figure 10.2 A common wave-like pattern of grief

has focused on what is considered to be 'normal' grief. By understanding the experience and trajectory of normal grief more fully, researchers and clinicians will be better able to identify complicated or prolonged grief reactions and develop effective interventions.

Wound analogy

Most people agree that grief needs to be expressed in some way, even though the best way of doing this depends considerably on people's personalities and communication styles. Many people find the 'wound analogy' helpful in understanding the importance of expressing their grief.

Imagine you have a large, infected wound on your leg that is causing you extreme pain and discomfort. It is deep and raw. The infection needs to be treated before the wound can begin to heal over, which possibly involves anti-biotic treatment or a daily dressing. Once the infection has gone and the wound starts to heal, it gradually becomes less tender and eventually you will be able to touch it without causing pain. But the wound remains marked by a scar, and you will always be able to recall the pain that was associated with the injury and the infection.

Even though this is a crude analogy, it demonstrates the need for someone who has been bereaved to find a way to express their grief. They might need to tell their story again and again in an attempt to make sense of what has happened. Or they might need to cry or ask difficult questions about their future. There is no right or wrong way to grieve. Some people will want to talk about their pain and loss while others may be very private and want to keep things to themselves. Neither way is better than the other. What's important is to let the person who is grieving take the lead. Don't try to push them to talk — just let them know you are there if they do feel like talking. Be prepared to hear them say the same thing again and again, and resist the urge to jump in with solutions or comments to 'correct' their statements. What they need is someone who can truly listen without offering opinions or judgements. Even though it may be tedious for you at times to keep hearing the same things over and over, this type of support is very useful. It helps the person who has been bereaved to begin to adapt to the changes that have been forced on them. As someone repeats their story they are able to express their pain, which at the same time helps them to reconcile the death in some way.

There is no right way to grieve. Let the person who has been bereaved take the lead.

A different path

A useful way to look at life is to think of all the different relationships we have with each other, with each one following its own path. When two people are in a relationship, irrespective of the type of relationship, the path they are taking together will be heading in a certain direction. And the path that a couple follows will be different to the path a parent and child takes for instance. Unfortunately when one person dies, the other is forced on to another path, not of their choosing. The original path on which they were travelling is no longer an option and the new path is different and unknown. Immediately following the death, the person who has been bereaved finds themself at a fork in their life's path. But rather than being able to choose where to go they are forced to take the unfamiliar path – the path without their loved one (see figure 9.1 in Chapter 9). Typically the greatest adjustment that someone has to make occurs in the first section of the new path, closest in time to the death of their loved one. It is here where they are likely to experience most of their ups and downs. The challenge they face as they move along this path is to make it as rewarding and enjoyable as possible, even though they would prefer to be back on their original path with their loved one.

Getting through the 'firsts'

When somebody experiences an event for the first time after the death of a loved one, it can be a significant moment. People often refer to these as 'firsts'. There will be many firsts – some can be anticipated such as a loved one's birthday, Christmas or the first anniversary of their death; others will come out of the blue, such as hearing a special song on the radio or receiving a letter addressed to the person who died. Often these firsts will cause somebody to experience an overwhelming sense of longing or pining for their loved one. And they can correlate with trigger waves on the wave-like pattern of grief. These reactions are normal and they don't mean that someone is getting 'worse'. Hopefully, as time goes on, each time someone experiences a first it will get a little easier to manage. You can provide much-needed support at times when known dates are approaching by helping the person who has been bereaved to make a plan to tackle the first. Chapter 8 introduced a framework for tackling firsts, which included four key components: anticipation, planning, realistic expectations, and reminiscing to maintain the connection with a loved one. If you are asked to provide support by helping someone manage a first, use exercise 8.3 in Chapter 8 to work through the process step by step.

After our son died it was so hard for everyone as no one expects a healthy 24-year-old to die. What we found really helped was that we would all go to his favourite pub each year on his birthday. It's become a bit of a tradition with his friends and for us it is a wonderful link to what might have been.

SUSAN, 53

Providing the best support

Depending on your relationship with the person who has been bereaved, there will be many different things you can do to support them through this difficult time. But it's often difficult to know what to say or how to behave, and some people end up saying or doing hurtful things quite unintentionally. Here are some of the most common 'hurts' mentioned by people who are grieving.

- Friends and colleagues failing to acknowledge the death
- Friends and family not calling when they said they would
- Insensitive comments such as, 'You've got to pull yourself together' (also see page 295)

If you want to provide the best support possible for someone who is grieving, follow these eight points. They are explained in detail below.

- Learn about grief
- Develop empathy
- Have patience
- Be a good listener
- Learn to sit with another's pain
- Don't tell, judge or compare
- Acknowledge significant dates
- Offer practical support

1. Learn about grief

Understanding the nature of grief will help you understand more fully the experience of someone who is grieving. Remember these main points.

- Grief is unique and tends to follow a wave-like pattern
- It is a normal and expected reaction to the death of a loved one
- Grief is not an illness
- It is characterised by yearning or pining for the person who has died

- Grief cannot be hurried or forced
- You cannot know another person's pain

2. Develop empathy

Empathy is one of the most important attributes to demonstrate when you are supporting someone who is grieving. *Empathy* is defined as 'understanding a person from his or her frame of reference rather than one's own, so that one vicariously experiences the person's feelings, perceptions, and thoughts'. Contrary to popular belief, empathy is not about imagining how you would behave or react in the same situation. It's about forgetting your own perspective, focusing on someone else's experience, and imagining what life is like for them at that point in time. Empathy allows you to accept what someone feels as their reality. It doesn't involve telling them how to think, feel or act. Some people are more empathic than others but it is a skill you can learn. To provide empathic support try to do the following.

- Really listen to what you are being told
- Resist the urge to offer solutions
- Be comfortable with silence
- Be comfortable with things that are difficult to hear
- Avoid bringing up similar experiences you know of, or have had

3. Have patience

It's not unusual to feel impatient at times with family or friends when they are grieving and this feeling can arise from two types of belief. First, that someone isn't progressing as quickly as you'd expect – that they should be 'better' by now. And second, that there is nothing that you can do to fix their problem, which causes you discomfort. If you are someone's main support and you notice that at times you become impatient, you need to develop back-up plans. Is there someone else who can help you? Do you need to suggest to the person who has been bereaved that they might need extra assistance, such as attending a support group or seeing a counsellor?

After my stepfather died my mother became fixated on his final weeks and nothing I suggested seemed to help. I tried and tried, but after a while I dreaded visiting her for fear of having to listen to the same old thing again and again. In the end I suggested that she should talk to her doctor about seeing a grief counsellor. Luckily for both of us she did and slowly she began to accept that he was gone.

GAYLE, 37

4. Be a good listener

This is harder to do than it sounds. Being a good listener means letting someone speak their mind without interrupting. It also means listening to every word they say and not thinking ahead to your next response. It means being fully present in the room – not letting your thoughts drift off to other things. People who are grieving often need to talk but they aren't always looking for answers – at least not someone else's answers. Talking is often the way they try to make sense of what has happened, which allows them to attempt to find their own answers. A common counselling skill is called 'active listening'. This is where the therapist listens closely and attentively to a client, asking questions where appropriate to fully understand the content of the message and the depth of the client's emotion. If you find that you are talking more than the person you are supporting, you need to ask yourself whether you are really listening.

5. Learn to sit with somebody's pain

You might be wondering what it actually means to sit with another person's pain. When somebody is grieving the death of a loved one, the only thing that would take their pain away is if their loved one came back to life. As this isn't possible there really is nothing anyone can do to make them feel better or 'back to normal'. The only thing that will help to ease their pain a little is unconditional support. Saying things that you hope will make them feel less pain often may just sound callous to the person who is grieving, even if they were well meant. The difficulty is that most people want to avoid pain at all costs. So the challenge to sit with another person's pain, without trying to 'fix' it, runs contrary to the desire to avoid pain. Sitting with somebody's pain means listening without saying or doing anything that suggests you want them to stop expressing their pain. If this is something you just can't do, you need to be able to acknowledge this to yourself and encourage the person who is grieving to seek this type of support elsewhere. Don't be hard on yourself if you can't offer this support. Instead think about what other types of support you can offer – you might be able to give practical support such as cooking or looking after the children.

> *When my friend's mother died under tragic circumstances,*
> *no one could do anything to ease her grief, other than just*
> *being there. All I could do was sit with her as she sobbed,*
> *give her the occasional hug and offer her food and drink.*

LIBBIE, 32

6. Don't tell, judge or compare

Even if you have experienced the death of a loved one or know of others who have, remember that everyone's grief is unique. So resist the urge to tell someone who has been bereaved what to do – it doesn't help. Too often people who are grieving are told that they should be doing certain things such as removing their loved one's belongings or taking off their wedding ring. It's important for people to make these decisions themselves and do what is right for them. With grief there are no rules about what should or shouldn't be done and no timescales. The only guideline health professionals suggest is that people who have been bereaved should avoid making major decisions in the first year, especially those that cannot be reversed. This is to encourage people not to make decisions based on emotion that they may regret at a later stage. It also doesn't help to tell other people's stories about grief in an effort to make someone feel better, unless they instigate this type of sharing themselves – for example in a bereavement group. Comments that suggest somebody's loss isn't as bad as someone else's, or that they should be over their loss by now, are not helpful and may be hurtful. Listed below are the types of comments to avoid when you're supporting someone who is grieving.

WHAT NOT TO SAY

- They had a good life
- At least you had them for as many years as you did
- You have to be thankful because they are at peace now
- They are in a better place now
- You're young, you can marry again
- You can have another baby
- You have to pull yourself together
- You have to think of the children
- You have to get over it
- You've got to stop crying
- You've got to get on with your life
- It's been six weeks, I thought you'd be better by now
- You've got to be strong
- You've got to snap out of it

- It was God's will
- I know how you feel
- You have to sort out their belongings immediately
- You should have gone back to work by now

SUGGESTION: WRITING SYMPATHY CARDS

Often people struggle with what to write in a sympathy card. It's hard to find the right words to let someone know you're thinking of them, while at the same time not implying that you know how they feel. Here are some suggestions that might give you some ideas.

- I am so sorry
- I was so sorry to hear about_____'s death
- Thinking of you
- I don't know what you are going through but I wanted you to know that I am thinking about you
- There are no words, other than to say how sorry we are
- Our thoughts are with you
- We are all thinking about you during this difficult time
- You and your family are in our thoughts and prayers

7. Acknowledge significant dates

As significant dates or events draw near, you might find that the person you are supporting withdraws. It is not uncommon for someone who is grieving to experience intense feelings of sadness, especially if the event is a 'first'. It can really help if you do something to remember the birthday of the person who died, or simply mention their name around a festive or holiday period. This helps the bereaved person because one of their fears is that their loved one will be forgotten. If possible try to make a note of significant dates so you can acknowledge them. You can send a card, an email or make a call. Mentioning that you're aware the date is approaching gives the bereaved person permission to raise the subject with you. The kind of approach that may work well is outlined below.

ACKNOWLEDGING SIGNIFICANT DATES OR EVENTS

Step 1. Send a clear message that you have remembered the date and that it's okay with you to talk about it. Being able to plan for these events helps someone who is grieving feel more in control when the day actually arrives. *I know it will be the first anniversary of _____ 's death next week. I know _____ 's birthday is coming up – are you planning to do anything on the day?*

Step 2. Offer to help with making plans. *Have you any plans? Would you like the two of us to do something on that day?*

Step 3. If the bereaved person is a little reluctant, you might want to be proactive and suggest the specifics of the invitation. *You can't say no – I'm going to pick you up at 11am and we can visit the cemetery first, and then I am going to take you out to lunch.*

But if they tell you that they don't want to go, you need to respect their wishes.

8. Offer practical support

When someone's grief is new it can be overwhelming for them to try to comprehend what has happened. Simple things are no longer simple and just getting through each hour can take all of their energy. Often in the early weeks there is an abundance of food and people dropping in to offer their condolences and support. But as time goes on and people's lives return to normal, the person who has been bereaved often feels more alone as the reality begins to sink in. If you want to give them some practical support it can be really helpful to do something on a regular basis such as running errands or picking up and dropping off children from their activities – it's one less thing they need to organise. It's best to offer your help in plain terms so that the other person doesn't have to make the request. Notice the difference between the following statements. *I will pick up the children and take them to soccer practice on Tuesday – that way you don't have to worry about them.* And, *Let me know if you want me to take the children to soccer practice on Tuesday.* Often people think they are offering support when they tell someone to call if they need something. But the reality is that most people won't call because they don't want to impose or won't remember the offer.

> *Offer help in plain terms so that the person who is*
> *grieving doesn't have to make the request.*
> *Don't leave the ball in their court.*

Next is a summary of the things you can do to help someone who is grieving.

GIVING GOOD SUPPORT – HOW BEST
TO HELP SOMEONE WHO HAS BEEN
BEREAVED

- Encourage them to tell their loved one's story
- Encourage them to tell their own story
- Listen without interrupting
- Acknowledge their feelings
- Accept their feelings without challenging them
- Sit with their pain

- Let them cry – tell them that sad doesn't mean bad
- Invite them to do things you think they would normally enjoy
- If you say you will call, make sure you do
- Avoid making promises that you can't keep
- Remember significant dates such as their loved one's birthday or the date they died
- Bring up the deceased person's name in conversation
- Reminisce with them
- Offer practical help such as cooking meals, shopping, babysitting and so on
- Suggest they see a counsellor if they appear to be having difficulty resuming some of their normal activities
- Offer to accompany them to first-time appointments to see the doctor, the lawyer and the bank for instance
- Offer to help write thank you notes for donations, flowers and sympathy cards
- Encourage them to re-establish their routine in some way
- Invite them to do something simple with you such as going for a walk or a drive

---

SUGGESTION: CHILDREN AND GRIEF

If the person who is grieving has children, they will need extra help – especially at the funeral and during the first few weeks when affairs need to be finalised. It's a good idea to assign a 'minder' to young children during the funeral, who can take them out of the service if they become restless. This way the person who has been bereaved does not need to worry about looking after the children. See Chapter 6 for more information.

As the first year goes on

For those supporting someone who is grieving, life returns to normal very quickly after the death. The busyness of life takes over and it's easy to forget to call and drop round as often as you did in the early days and weeks. But for the person who is grieving, life is forever changed by the death of their loved one. And when others begin to contact them less often, their feelings of isolation and loneliness grow even stronger. The void in their life becomes more apparent and it often feels to them as though things are getting worse, not better – especially in the early months. So be mindful that for the person who has been bereaved there are no time limits for their grief. Realistically, until they have passed the first anniversary of their loved one's death, they have not experienced all the typical firsts. There will be other firsts after the first anniversary but most people report that getting through this first is a significant milestone. Hopefully as each month passes, they will begin to build their life's new path and find enjoyment and a sense of purpose again.

For those dealing with the death of a child, their grief tends to be more intense and lasts much longer. If you are supporting someone who has lost a child, anticipate significant firsts in years to come, such as when their child would have graduated from high school or gone to university. These are significant milestones that are often not acknowledged, adding to a parent's heartache.

SUGGESTION: WHEN TO SUGGEST PROFESSIONAL HELP

There might be situations where you are really concerned about the well-being of your friend or family member, especially if they don't seem to be accepting that their life has changed. If you are concerned then encourage them to seek help. Look back to 'A note of caution' at the beginning of *Overcoming Grief* for the list of warning signs that need to be taken seriously. You will find information on how to seek professional help in Appendix 3. If you believe your loved one is at risk of harming themselves or they have expressed thoughts of suicide, then seek help immediately by either taking them to the emergency room at your local hospital or contacting their doctor.

SUGGESTION: SUPPORT GROUPS

It might be possible to find a specific type of support group, depending on who died and the circumstances of their death. Examples where a specific type of group is recommended include the death of a child, deaths resulting from suicide, sudden infant death and homicide. Some organisations also run widow/widower groups and hospices usually offer a variety of bereavement support groups. You will find contact details for a number of different types of support organisations in Appendix 3.

Why we need to improve society's understanding of grief

Death affects everyone at some stage in life, often many times over. Yet it is a subject that many people try to avoid. The best thing that we can do to help support people who have been bereaved, as well as ourselves, is to become

303

more comfortable with death. For too long people have considered death and dying taboo subjects. Often people don't want to draw up a will or select guardians for their children in case they jinx themselves. If death was discussed more openly in families and in schools, people would begin to see it for what it really is – another part of life. If, on an individual level, everybody improved their understanding of grief just a little more then society would gradually become better equipped to support those who are grieving as they struggle with their heartache. The expectation that grief should be over in an instant does everyone a huge disservice. This belief needs to be challenged and replaced with a more realistic expectation. Try to remember that *grief affects everyone in a different way. It is not an illness with a cure but a process of adjustment, which makes it impossible to predict how long it will continue.*

TIPS TO IMPROVE YOUR UNDERSTANDING OF GRIEF

These suggestions are for both individuals and different organisations such as schools, universities and community groups. They will help you learn more about the topics of dying, death and grief.

- Contact a local hospice to see if it offers any presentations about caring for people who are terminally ill and those dealing with grief

- Seek out resource materials (books, DVDs) about death and grief
- Contact a local funeral home and ask for information – some may even allow you to visit
- Contact professionals who deal with death and grief and invite them to visit your group. Try approaching doctors, nurses, hospital chaplains, ministers or other clergy, hospice staff and undertakers for their different perspectives on these subjects

Preparing for death and grief

You may have had a lot of experience of death and grief or you may have never experienced the death of a loved one. One of the hardest things in life is preparing for grief. Many people would prefer to avoid any thought or discussion about death at all. But the problem with this is that unfinished business often makes it harder for people who have been bereaved. It is impossible to predict how anyone will react when a significant loved one dies. But there are some things that you can do ahead of time to help your loved ones and yourself.

1. Draw up a will and arrange your affairs, which includes assigning guardians for your children.
2. Don't wait to tell your loved ones how much they mean to you. Tell them now.

3. Be clear about what treatments and interventions you would or wouldn't want performed if you were seriously ill. Make a 'living will' to set out your instructions.

4. Assign a person to make these decisions for you if you become unable to make these decisions for yourself.

5. Be clear about your wishes after your death regarding your funeral, organ donation and burial/cremation.

6. Record your hopes for your loved ones and how you envisage their lives continuing without you.

As you continue to support your family member, friend or colleague as they grieve, be mindful of how you might not only help them but also how you can help shape the way society approaches end-of-life issues. Everyone needs to become more comfortable with the subjects of death, dying and grief. Just as you take an active role in managing your physical health, your children's education or your retirement plans, you need to start attending to your end-of-life care by bringing these topics out into the open. Death and grief affects everyone in one way or another. Given that we can never know exactly how our story or the stories of those closest to us will end, it is important to ask *how can we prepare?*

Summary

- Everyone grieves in their own way
- Allow someone to express their pain

- Let them take the lead
- Avoid telling them what to do
- Acknowledge significant dates
- Offer practical support
- Prepare for death and grief in your own life

Appendix 1

Keeping a journal

Many people who are grieving find it very therapeutic to write in a journal. Not only does writing provide a way to express your thoughts and feelings about the death of your loved one and how your life is changing, but it also helps you maintain a connection with them. Even if you find the concept of writing unfamiliar, it's worth trying because it is another way to deal with your loss. Plus it is something that you can do privately and readily. Writing down your thoughts and feelings is a powerful tool because it takes more cognitive processing actually to put pen to paper than just to think things through. It also allows you to track your progress as you come to terms with the death of your loved one. You can write about anything, but here are a few suggestions.

- Your thoughts about your loved one's death
- Their absence
- Your feelings
- How your life has changed and continues to change
- Different memories
- The things you didn't get a chance to say

There are no rules. Often people find great benefit in just being able to express their thoughts and feelings. You might find at first that writing to your loved one is overwhelming. You might even want to stop because you fear you are getting worse. These are normal reactions. What is probably happening is that writing is tapping into these thoughts and feelings in a more focused way. Take your time, remind yourself that it is okay to cry, and stick with the feelings for as long as you can. In time you will find that they ease.

Getting started

If you don't already have a special journal then you might like to buy a blank book or diary that has special meaning to you – maybe it's a special colour or has a picture on the cover that reminds you of your loved one. Alternatively you could use a loose-leaf folder and make your own cover. When you're ready to begin, find a place where you won't be disturbed. Make sure that you build in enough time afterwards in case you are exhausted or want to be alone. Some people like to play music while they write or light a candle. Others prefer to write outdoors. It's important to find somewhere that works for you.

Suggestions for journal entries

There are many ways to start an entry. You could write each one as a letter to your loved one. Or you could just write down your thoughts as they come, without much structure or order. Another suggestion is to write about the emotion that best describes how you are feeling at the time – for instance sad, pining, guilty, disbelieving, relieved, angry, peaceful and so on (see table 2.1 for a list).

Here is a list of phrases and sentences that will also give you some ideas about how to start.

- It's been _____ days/weeks/months since you died
- I wish I could . . .
- If you were here now, I would . . .
- Before you died, I wish I had been able to tell you . . .
- I want to tell you what I've been doing
- I want to ask your advice about something
- I want to tell you how I have been feeling
- I regret that I didn't . . .
- I am angry about . . .
- I miss your . . .
- The hardest things are . . .
- I didn't expect that I would feel . . .
- I think about what you would say to me now. I think you would want me to . . .
- This time last year we were . . .
- It's your birthday today and I wanted to tell you . . .
- I saw a grief counsellor today. I talked about . . . Afterwards I felt . . .
- I attended a support group today. Afterwards I felt . . . and thought . . .
- I am trying to . . .
- My life is different now. I know you would tell me to . . .

- I am trying to do things to lessen grief's hold on me.
  I am . . .

These are only a few suggestions. You will probably think of others once you start writing. Set aside a regular time to write, or write whenever you feel the need. Most people find that over time they write less often. Remember to date your entries so you can look back over what you have written and see the progress you have made.

Appendix 2

Useful frameworks

Framework for challenging unhelpful thoughts

This framework can be used to help you challenge any unhelpful thoughts that are causing strong, negative emotions and/or destructive behaviour. Whenever you experience a negative emotion, use the thought diary format (see page 319) to challenge your thinking and generate new, helpful thoughts, which in turn will help change the way you feel.

THOUGHT DIARY FORMAT

A	B	C	D	E
Situation or trigger	Unhelpful thoughts	Feelings (score/10) Behaviour	Helpful thoughts	New feelings (score/10) New behaviour

Step 1. Write down the situation, event or trigger in (A). It may be a memory of an event.

Step 2. Identify the main feeling or emotion you're experiencing and record this in (C) along with any unhelpful behaviours you've noticed. Rate the intensity of your feeling or emotion on a scale of 0–10, with 10 being the greatest or the strongest.

Step 3. Articulate the thought behind this feeling or emotion and record it in (B).

Step 4. Challenge your unhelpful thoughts using these five questions.

    1. Where's the evidence for what I thought in (B)?

    2. What are the alternatives to what I thought in (B)?

3. What is the likely effect on me of thinking in this way?
4. How would I advise a friend to think in the same situation?
5. What would my loved one tell me to do if they were here now?

Step 5. Rewrite your new, helpful thoughts in (D) using your answers to these questions.

Step 6. Identify the new feeling or emotion. Rate the intensity of your new emotion on a scale of 0–10 as you did in step 2. If you recorded a behaviour in (C), is there now a new behaviour that is constructive? In (E) record your new feeling and its rating, along with your new behaviour.

Framework for making difficult decisions

This framework can be used to help you make any decision you are facing. By working through each step you are less likely to make an impulsive decision based on emotion.

Step 1.   What is the problem you are experiencing or the decision you are facing?

Step 2.   How many possible solutions can you list?

Step 3.   What are the positives and negatives of each of these possible solutions?

Step 4.   Which looks best to you?

Step 5.   If you used this solution, what would the consequences be?

Step 6.   Can you live with these consequences? Yes/No

Step 7.   If you answered 'no' in step 6, go back to step 2 and work through the remaining steps again.

Step 8.   If you use the solution you identified in step 4, what action do you need to take to try this solution out?

Framework for tackling avoidance

This framework outlines the steps you need to take to tackle gradually situations that you may have been avoiding or approaching with great difficulty.

Step 1. What places are you avoiding?

Step 2. What people are you avoiding?

Step 3. What activities are you avoiding?

Step 4. For each item you listed above, what do you fear would happen if you didn't avoid them?

Step 5. Rank the items you listed in steps 1–3, starting with the easiest to confront.

Step 6. For each one, write down what you think about the item you are avoiding.

Step 7. Challenge any unhelpful or self-defeating thoughts using the five questions below. Write down your new, helpful thoughts.

1. Where's the evidence for what I thought?
2. What are the alternatives to what I thought?

---

3. What is the likely effect on me of thinking in this way?

4. How would I advise a friend to think in the same situation?

5. What would my loved one tell me to do if they were here now?

Step 8. Plan how you can gradually approach the items you are avoiding, beginning with the least difficult. If possible break down each item into smaller steps, beginning with the least difficult step.

USEFUL FRAMEWORKS

A	B	C	D	E
Situation or trigger	Unhelpful thoughts	Feelings (score/10) Behaviour	Helpful thoughts	New feelings (score/10) New behaviour

Appendix 3

Resources

Finding professional help

If you are dealing with the death of a loved one and want professional help, consult a therapist, counsellor or psychologist who is experienced in grief counselling. To find a suitable professional try the following:

1. Ask your doctor or GP to refer you to a licensed therapist who deals with grief.
2. Contact your national hospice organisation to find a hospice in your area that provides bereavement support.
3. Contact your national psychological association for a list of registered psychologists in your area.
4. Ask your friends and family to recommend a therapist.

THIS IS A LIST OF ORGANISATIONS THAT CAN
PROVIDE INFORMATION ABOUT GRIEF AND
HOW TO GET PROFESSIONAL HELP

UK

**British Association for Behavioural and Cognitive
Psychotherapies (BABCP)**
Tel: 0161 705 4304
Email: babcp@babcp.com
www.babcp.com

**British Association for Counselling and
Psychotherapy**
Tel: 01455 883300
Email: bacp@bacp.co.uk
www.bacp.co.uk

The British Psychological Society
Tel: 0116 254 9568
Email: enquiry@bps.org.uk
www.bps.org.uk

Campaign Against Drinking and Driving
Tel: 0845 123 5541 or 0845 123 5543
Helpline: 0845 123 5542
Email: cadd@scard.org.uk
www.cadd.org.uk

Childhood Bereavement Network
Tel: 020 7843 6309
Email: cbn@ncb.org.uk
www.childhoodbereavementnetwork.org.uk

Child Bereavement Charity
Tel: 01494 568900 (Support and Information service)
Helpline: 0800 02 88840
Email: support@childbereavementuk.org
www.childbereavementuk.org

The Child Death Helpline
Helpline: 0800 282 986/0808 800 6019
Email: contact@childdeathhelpline.org
www.childdeathhelpline.org.uk

Great Ormond Street Hospital Child Death Helpline
Great Ormond Street Hospital for Children NHS Trust
Bereavement Services Department: 020 7813 8551
www.gosh.nhs.uk

The Compassionate Friends (UK)
(For bereaved parents and their families following the
death of a child)
Tel: 0345 120 3785
Helpline: 0345 123 2304
0288 77 88 016 (NI)
Email: info@tcf.org.uk and helpline@tcf.org.uk
www.tcf.org.uk

Counselling Directory
www.counselling-directory.org.uk

Cruse Bereavement Care
Helpline: 0808 808 1677
Email: www.cruse.org.uk

Northern Ireland
Tel: 028 90 792419
Email: northern.ireland@cruse.org.uk

Scotland
Tel: 01738 444 178
Helpline: 0845 600 2227
www.crusescotland.org.uk

Northern Ireland – Department of Health, Social Services and Public Safety
Tel: 028 9052 0500
www.dhsspsni.gov.uk

Directgov
(Online portal for government services)
www.direct.gov.uk

Wales – Welsh Assembly Government
Tel: 0300 060440
Email: customerhelp@gov.wales
www.gov.wales/topics/health/?lang=en

Scotland – The Scottish Government Health and Social Care
Tel: 0300 244 4000
Email: ceu@gov.scot
www.gov.scot/topics/health

Help the Hospices
Tel: 020 7520 8200
Email: info@hospiceuk.org
www.hospiceuk.org

The Jewish Bereavement Counselling Service
Tel: 0208 951 3881
Email: enquiries@jbcs.org.uk
www.jbcs.org.uk

The Ruby Care Foundation
(Support for families before and after the death of a
terminally ill loved one)
Tel: 0333 011 7556
Email: info@rubycare.org
www.rubycare.org

The Samaritans (24-hour support)
Tel: 116123
Email: jo@samaritans.org
www.samaritans.org

SANDS – Stillbirth & neonatal death charity
Tel: 0808 164 3332
Email: helpline@sands.org.uk
www.uk-sands.org

USA

International Association for Hospice and Palliative Care
Tel: +1 346 571 5919
Toll Free: +1 866 374 2472
www.hospicecare.com

Aging with Dignity (End of Life Information)
Tel: +1 850 681 2010
Email: fivewishes@agingwithdignity.org
www.agingwithdignity.org

American Association of Retired Persons (AARP)
Tel: +1 888 OUR AARP (+1 888 687 2277)
www.aarp.org

American Foundation for Suicide Prevention
Toll Free: 888 333 AFSP (2377)
Tel: +1 212 363 3500
Crisis line: +1 800 273 TALK (+1 800 273 8255)
Email: info@afsp.org
www.afsp.org

The American Psychological Association
Tel: +1 800 374 2721 or +1 202 336 5500
www.apa.org

The Children's Room
1210 Massachusetts Avenue
Arlington MA 02476
Tel: +1 781 641 4741
Email: info@childrensroom.org
www.childrensroom.org

The Compassionate Friends, Inc.
(For bereaved parents and their families following the death of a child)
Toll Free: 877 969 0010
Tel: +1 630 990 0010
www.compassionatefriends.org

The Dougy Center for Grieving Children & Families
PO Box 86852
Portland OR 97286
Tel: +1 503 775 5683
Toll Free: 866 775 5683
Email: help@dougy.org
www.dougy.org

The Good Grief Program
(Child bereavement)
Boston Medical Center, Boston MA 02118
Tel: +1 617 414 4005
www.bmc.org/programs/good-grief-program

Hospice Foundation of America
Tel: +1 800 854 3402
www.hospicefoundation.org

The National Hospice & Palliative Care Organization
Tel: +1 703 837 1500
nhpco_info@nhpco.org
www.nhpco.org

CANADA

Canadian Hospice Palliative Care Association
Info Line: +1 877 203 4636
Tel: +1 613 241 3663 or 1 800 668 2785
www.chpca.net

The Canadian Psychological Association
141 Laurier Avenue West, Suite 702
Ottawa ON K1P 5J3
Toll free: +1 888 472 0657
Tel: +1 613 237 2144
Fax: +1 613 237 1674
Email: cpa@cpa.ca
www.cpa.ca

AUSTRALIA

Australian Centre for Grief and Bereavement

Tel: +61 3 9265 2100
Freecall: 1800 642 066
Email: info@grief.org.au
www.grief.org.au

The Australian Psychological Society

Toll free: 1800 333 497
Tel: +61 3 8662 3300
Email: contactus@psychology.org.au
www.psychology.org.au

Bereavement Care Centre

(Support for the terminally ill and bereaved)
Tel: 1300 654 556 and +61 2 9804 6909
Email: info@bereavementcare.com.au
www.bereavementcare.com.au

Palliative Care Australia

Tel: +61 2 6232 0700
Email: pcainc@palliativecare.org.au
www.palliativecare.org.au

NEW ZEALAND

The New Zealand Psychological Society

Tel: + 64 4 473 4884
www.psychology.org.nz

Hospice New Zealand
Tel: + 64 4 381 0266
www.hospice.org.nz

GENERAL WEBSITES

www.caringinfo.org
www.centeringcorp.com
www.childrengrieve.org
www.griefnet.org
www.growthhouse.org

References

'The pain of the grief is being felt to its full extent.' Page 16

Adapted from discussions in *Coping with Grief* (see Further Reading) about the chemicals the body releases following the news of a death.

Exercise 2.2 Writing with your other hand. Page 26

Adapted from *Six Simple Weeks – A Caring Manual for Support Group Leaders*, E. Cole and J. Johnson, Centering Corporation (2001). Used with permission.

'Research shows that crying helps rid the body of stress-induced chemicals.' Page 35

Refers to the work of biochemist William Frey in *Crying, The Mystery of Tears*, W. Frey, Harpers and Row (1985).

Exercise 4.4 Framework for challenging unhelpful thoughts. Page 78

Questions 1–4 are taken from *Online and Personal: the Reality of Internet Relationships*, J. Lamble and S. Morris,

Finch Publishing (2001), which are based on discussions in *Mind Over Mood – Change How You Feel By Changing the Way You Think,* D. Greenberger and C. Padesky, Guildford Press (1995); and in *The Treatment of Anxiety Disorders,* G. Andrews, R. Crino, C. Hunt, L. Lampe and A. Page, Cambridge University Press (1994). Question 5 is an extension of techniques commonly used by grief counsellors.

Exercise 5.2 A Framework for making difficult decisions. Page 113

Adapted from 'The framework for making choices' in *Motherhood: Making it Work for You,* J. Lamble and S. Morris, Finch Publishing (1999).

Table 6.1 Children's understanding of death at different ages. Page 140

Adapted from the work of Maria Trozzi and Deborah Rivlin from *The Good Grief Program* of Boston Medical Center. See www.bmc.org

Guidelines for talking to children about death. Page 146

This list is developed from my work with clients and the advice offered in *Coping with Grief* (see Further Reading) and *The Good Grief Program* of Boston Medical Center (see above).

'To be truly empathic.' Page 172

Adapted from *The Partner Test: How Well are the Two of You Suited?* J. Lamble and S. Morris, Finch Publishing (2004).

'The stage theory of grief.' Page 284

See *An Empirical Examination of the Stage Theory of Grief* (see Further Reading).

Further reading

DEFINITIONS

For definitions of grief, hope, empathy and active listening see *APA Dictionary of Psychology*, G. R. VandenBos (Ed.), American Psychological Association (2007).

For a fuller explanation of the 'flight or fight' response and a helpful guide to dealing with anxiety problems, see *Overcoming Anxiety – A Self-Help Guide Using Cognitive Behavioural Techniques*, 2nd Edition, H. Kennerley, Robinson (2015).

For clinical definitions of pining and yearning see *The Macquarie Dictionary*, A. Delbridge (Ed.), The Macquarie Library Pty Ltd (1990).

COGNITIVE BEHAVIOURAL THERAPY

Cognitive Therapy and the Emotional Disorders, A. T. Beck, New York University Press (1976). A useful guide to the principles of cognitive behavioural therapy.

GRIEF AND LOSS

An Empirical Examination of the Stage Theory of Grief, P. Maciejewski, B. Zhang, S. Block and H. Prigerson, *Journal of the American Medical Association*, 297(7):716–723 (2007).

Coping with Grief, M. McKissock, Australian Broadcasting Corporation (1995). Also see www.bereavementcare. com.au.

Dying Well: Peace and Possibilities at the End of Life, I. Byock, Riverhead Books (1997).

Final Gifts: Understanding the Special Awareness, Needs and Communications of the Dying, M. Callanan and P. Kelley, Bantam Books (2012).

Grief Counseling and Grief Therapy. A Handbook for the Mental Health Practitioner, J. W. Worden, J. W. Springer Publishing Company (1991).

Grieving: How to go on Living when Someone You Love Dies, T. A. Rando, Bantam Books (1991).

Handbook of Bereavement: Theory, Research, and Intervention, M. Stroebe, W. Stroebe and R. Hansson (Eds.), Cambridge University Press (1993).

Handbook of Bereavement, Research and Practice: Advances in Theory and Intervention, M. S. Stroebe, R. O. Hansson, H. Schut and W. Stroebe (Eds.), American Psychological Association (2008).

Handbook of Thanatology: The Essential Body of Knowledge for the

Study of Death, Dying, and Bereavement, D. K. Meagher and D. E. Balk (Eds.), Routledge (2013).

Helping Bereaved Parents: A Clinician's Guide, R. Tedeschi and L. Calhoun, Brunner-Routledge (2004).

Lessons of Loss: A Guide to Coping, R. Neimeyer, Center for the Study of Loss and Transition (2000).

Losing a Parent: Practical Help for you and Other Family Members, F. Marshall, Da Capo Press (2000).

No Time for Goodbyes: Coping with Sorrow, Anger and Injustice After a Tragic Death, J. Lord, Compassion Press (2014).

The Four Things that Matter Most: A Book About Living, I. Byock, Free Press (2014).

Widow to Widow: Thoughtful, Practical Ideas for Rebuilding your Life, G. D. Ginsburg, Da Capo Press (1997).

CHILDREN AND DEATH

Fire in my Heart, Ice in my Veins: A Journal for Teenagers Experiencing Loss, E. Samuel-Traisman, Centering Corporation (1992).

Helping Children Cope with Death, The Dougy Center, The Dougy Center for Grieving Children (2004). Also see www.dougy.org for other titles

Lifetimes: The Beautiful Way to Explain Death to Children, B. Mellonie and R. Ingpen, Bantam Books (1998).

Never Too Young to Know: Death in Children's Lives, P. Silverman, Oxford University Press (2000).

Talking with Children About Loss: Words, Strategies, and Wisdom to Help Children Cope with Death, Divorce, and Other Difficult Times, M. Trozzi and K. Massimini, A Perigee Book (1999).

What on Earth Do You Do When Someone Dies? T. Romain, Free Spirit Publishing Inc. (2003).

When Dinosaurs Die: A Guide to Understanding Death, L. Brown and M. Brown, Brown and Co. (1996).

Index

Page numbers in *italics* refer to Figures and Tables

action 101–37
  decision-making 112–16, 184–5, 316
  distraction 103
  eating well 106–8
  establishing/re-establishing routines 103, 104–6
  'just do it' 103, 104, 106, 222, 264–5
  loneliness, dealing with 121–2
  personal stories 102, 104, 106, 110
  physical exercise 106, 109–10, 111
  returning to work 117–19
  seeking help 132–6
  small steps 70, 100, 102, 243
  tackling avoidance 122–9, 317–18
  targeting losses 119–21
  'tool box' approach 10, 129–32
  unwillingness to act 101–2
active listening 293
adjustment 4, 6, 27, 29, 250, 257, 282
adrenaline 16
alcohol x, 63, 109, 111, 133
Alzheimer's disease 216
anger
  challenging unhelpful thoughts 84–9
  personal stories 73, 86, 89
  towards medical staff 85–6
  writing letters to express 88

anniversaries 207–44, 297–8
  anticipation of 212–13, 220
  birthdays 231–2, 289
  of death 217–21
  examples of 208–10
  festive holidays 221–31
  first year 22, 36, 37, 58, 207, 208–12
  firsts that never came 234–6, 302
  framework for tackling 212–17
  personal stories 211, 214–15, 217, 218, 219, 220–1, 224–5, 227, 230, 232, 235, 236, 237, 238–9
  planning for 213–15, 220
  realistic expectations 215, 220, 226–7
  reminiscing 216–17, 220
  support during 288–9, 297–8, 302
  unexpected firsts 237–43
  wedding and relationships 232–4
antidepressant medication 18
anxiety 18, 28
  medication 19
assertiveness about your own needs 8, 60, 167, 170, 174, 205, 228
automatic pilot 15–16
avoidance behaviour x
  personal stories 122–3, 124–5, 128
  tackling 122–9, 317–18

barriers to working through your
   grief 72–5
 anger 73, 84–9
 beliefs about fairness 72
 difficult relationships 90–2
 guilt 14, 72–3, 80–2, 83
 regret 73–4, 89–90
 unanswered questions 92–8
beliefs about the world, challenges to
   20–1, 72
birthdays 231–2, 289

caffeine 111
cemetery, visiting 182–3
change
 acknowledging losses 6, 45–6, 50
 death and 40–2, 44
Chanukah 227
children 138–62
 allowing them to say goodbye 154
 breaking the news to 143–4,
   147–51
 death of a child 17–18, 20, 21, 48,
   55, 94, 98, 183, 204–5, 218,
   234, 236, 260, 267, 302
 death of a parent 8, 47–8, 139–40,
   150, 160, 202–3
 expressions of grief 139–41, 157
 family rituals and traditions,
   encouraging 161
 guardians 304, 305
 healthy role-modelling about
   grieving 155, 157
 keeping the school informed
   152–3
 learning about grief 36
 memory books 198–9
 ongoing conversations 158–60
 personal stories 8–9, 17–18, 48,
   94, 98, 139–40, 147–8, 150,
   152, 157, 160, 161–2, 218,
   260, 267
 preparing them for the funeral
   150–1, 153–4, 156
 puberty 161
 regressive behaviours 139
 separated/divorced parents 160
 stillborn and miscarried children
   50, 204–5, 238–9
 support groups 159
 supporting bereaved children
   158–62, 202–3, 301
 talking about death to 142–7,
   158–9, 161
 talking about the future to 67
 teenagers 160–1
 understanding of death 140–1
Christmas 224–5, 229, 230
cognitive behavioural therapy (CBT)
   10, 75
comfort eating 108
concentration difficulties 28
control
 feeling a loss of 5, 7, 17–18, 280
 regaining 7, 17, 24–5, 42, 46, 52,
   63–100, 212, 213, 280
counselling 54, 55, 63, 93, 104, 128,
   135–6, 259
couples grieving 55
creative outlets 53
crying
 allowing yourself to 34, 35, 52,
   225–6
 crying easily 28, 34
 personal stories 34
 release of pain 35

dates, significant see anniversaries
death
 finality of, coming to terms with
   12
 preparation for 305–6
 taboo subject 304
 unexpected 14, 20, 45, 49, 72,
   93–4, 200–1
 violent 20, 73, 151, 191–2
 your wishes after 306
death rattle 95
decision-making
 avoiding major decisions in early
   days 258, 294–5
 difficult decisions 183–7, 316
 framework for making 112–16,
   184–5, 316

degenerative illnesses 216
depression x, 18, 133
  clinical 18, 19–20
difficult conversations 138–74
  with adults 162–73
  at work 163
  with children 138–62
  planning what you want to say
    163, 164–5
  using email 163, 164
difficult relationships 34, 253
  personal stories 92
  reconciling 50–1, 90–2
distraction 103
doctor, seeing your 18–19
dreams and nightmares 9, 28
duration of grief 15, 30, 36–7
dying, entertaining thoughts of 28,
  97

early days 12–17
  automatic pilot 15–16
  intensification of grief 16–17
  personal stories 16–17
  physical and emotional reactions
    13–14, 28
eating healthily 106–8
emotions
  gendered expression of 55
  loss of control 28
  suppression 43, 51
empathy 171–2, 291
end-of-life care 306
estate, dealing with the 114–16
exercise, physical 106, 109–10, 111
exercises
  anniversaries 211, 217, 219–20
  approaching difficult conversations
    166–7
  creating a memory book 196–7
  developing new connections with
    your loved one 190
  establishing routines 105
  facing wedding and relationship
    anniversaries 234
  filling your worry boxes 65, 66
  identifying barriers to grief 74

informing children about a death
  147
loss of roles 47
lowering expectations about festive
  holidays 227
making difficult decisions 113, 187
making sense of 'whys' 99
the other side of your grief 249
permission to cry 225–6
planning a statement about the
  death of a loved one 164–5
preparing for a specific day 120–1
reconciling difficult relationships
  91–2
remembering with a smile 192–3
scheduling and structuring 'grief
  time' 52–3
setting future goals 266
tackling avoidance behaviour
  123–4, 128
tackling guilt in a new relationship
  271
thoughts that keep you stuck,
  challenging 252–3
to-do lists 71
'tool box' items 130–1
trying new things 262
unanswered questions 94–5
unexpected firsts, coping with
  239–41
unhelpful beliefs about bereaved
  people 33
unhelpful thoughts, challenging
  78–80, 83
wave-like pattern of grief 25
what would your loved one want
  for you? 263–4
writing to your loved one 56–7
writing with your other hand 26–8
your own experiences of death and
  grief 277
expectations about grief 30–2, 280–1
  unrealistic 31, *32, 283*

faith and spirituality 96
family traditions, creating 161, 202,
  223–4, 230, 234–5

festive holiday seasons 221–31
'fight or flight' response 16
first year 208–12
  see also anniversaries
forgetting, anxiety about 175, 176–7
former self, feeling like 265
funeral, preparing children for
    150–1, 153–4, 156
fuzzy head 28

goodbye letters 155
grief
  analogies 29, 43, 133, 285–6
  children's expression of 139–41,
    157
  complexity of 4, 6, 41, 44, 46, 178,
    284–5
  definition of 2, 275–6
  duration 15, 30, 36–7
  expectations about 30–2, 280–1
  expressing 50–1
  healthy grieving 6, 35, 37, 39, 42–3
  life of its own 32, 60
  normal response 34, 281
  other side of 246–55
  patterns of *see* wave-like pattern
    of grief
  realistic beliefs about 35–6
  stage theory of 284–5
  uniqueness of 5–6, 43, 276–7, 294
'grief time', scheduling 51–4, 56,
    83, 178
guilt 14, 72–3, 230
  challenging 80–2, 83
  new relationships 268, 269–71
  personal stories 73, 269

happiness, rediscovering 230–1, 246–7
healthy grieving 6, 35, 37, 39, 42–3
hope 246–9
hopelessness x, 20, 133, 256
hospice care 73, 80, 95, 304
house, selling/not selling 114–16,
    183–7

illness, prolonged 14, 44, 45, 46,
    200, 201

journal, keeping a 10–11, 53, 54, 56,
    309–12
  personal stories 57–9
  suggestions for entries 310–12
  suggestions for topics 309–10
  thought diary 78–80

keepsakes 177, 179

legal and financial affairs 64, 67
lethargy 28
listening to the bereaved 292–3
living wills 306
living without the loved one 6
  see also paths, new
loneliness 121–2
loss
  acknowledging 45–6, 50, 51
  and change 27, 29, 40–2, 44, 45–6,
    277–80
  personal stories 40, 41, 46, 48, 49,
    50, 289
  roles, change or loss of 46, 47
  sexual relationship 48–9
loving again 268

maintaining connections with a
    loved one 175–206
  bereaved children 202–3
  creating new connections 178,
    188–91
  death of a child 204–5
  forgetting, anxiety about 175,
    176–7
  memories 192–9
  personal belongings 176, 177,
    178–80
  personal stories 176–7, 180, 181,
    183–4, 190–1, 200–1, 205
  selling/keeping the home 183–7
  suggestions 199–200
  telling their story 191–2
  visiting the cemetery 182–3
  wedding rings 180–1
medication 18–19
memories
  asking others 196, 198, 199, 203

creating a memory book 195–7
   positive 192–3
   reminiscing 216–17, 220, 229
   uncomfortable 194
memory book 53, 195–9
   children's memory books 198–9
mind, fears of losing your 28
miscarried babies 50, 205
moving forward 249–56
   feeling stuck 250–5
   seeking professional help 255–6
music 52, 110, 233

new relationships 268–72
numbness 12

orphaned adults 237–8
other people
   unhelpful/unrealistic beliefs and
      advice 33, 60, 61, 129, 162,
      165–6, 169, 278–9, 281, 295–6
   see also difficult conversations; sup-
      porting those grieving; work

paths, new 59, 243, 245–74, 257,
   287–8
   feeling like your former self 265
   hope 246–9
   identity, re-examining 267
   making it the best it can be 265–6
   moving forward 249–56
   new relationships 269–72
   personal stories 248–9, 260, 262–3,
      264, 265, 269, 271–2
   realistic expectations 256–8
   realistic goals 265–6
   support system 258–9
   trying new things 261–3
   what would your loved one want?
      263–4
patience 32, 41, 44, 229, 243,
   292
permission to grieve, giving yourself
   32, 34–5, 39–62, 225–6
personal belongings
   giving away 176, 179, 180
   keepsakes 177, 179

sorting through 178–80
photographs 53, 200
pining and yearning 13, 15, 24,
   28, 29–30, 122, 212, 288
professional help
   resources 320–9
   when to seek ix–x, 132–3, 255–6,
      302–3
   see also counselling
prolonged grief 20

racing thoughts 19, 72
regaining control 7, 17, 24–5, 42,
   46, 52, 63–100
   challenging unhelpful thoughts
      75–83, 231, 251–2
   dealing with unanswered questions
      92–8
   identifying barriers to grief 72–5
   sorting and prioritising worries
      64–8
   'to do' lists 69–71
   see also exercises
regret 73–4, 89–90
relief, sense of 14
remembering your loved one see
   memories; memory book
roles, change or loss of 46, 47
routines, establishing/re-establishing
   26, 104–6
rumination x

sadness
   giving yourself permission to feel
      sad 32, 34–5
   normality of 34, 35, 39
self-talk 218, 228, 261
sexual relationship, loss of 48–9
'should' statements 182
sleep
   disturbance x, 16, 18, 19, 110–12,
      133
   sleeping medication 19, 110
stage theory of grief 284–5
stillborn children 204–5, 238–9
suicidal thoughts x, 20, 133, 256,
   302–3

suicide 93, 96
  informing a child about 151–2
Sundays, coping with 119–21
support groups 1–2, 132, 173, 259, 303
  for children 159
  for teenagers 161
supporting those grieving 258–9, 275–307
  being a good listener 292–3
  being patient 292
  bereaved parents 302
  don't tell, judge or compare 294–5
  empathic support 171–2, 291
  'fix it' mentality 281, 282, 293
  learning about grief 290–1, 304–5
  learning to sit with somebody's pain 293–4
  letting the grieving person take the lead 286–7
  personal stories 292, 294
  practical support 298–9
  suggesting professional help 302–3
  supporting children 301
  sympathy cards 296
  through the 'firsts' 288–9, 297–8, 302
  unhelpful advice and comments 33, 60, 61, 129, 162, 165–6, 169, 278–9, 281, 295–6
  unintentional 'hurts' 289
sympathy cards 69, 296

talk
  the need to 2, 3–4, 286, 293
  preferring not to 4, 286
  story, telling your 50, 60, 286–7
thinking too far ahead 72
thought diary 78–80
time, passage of 25–6, 36–7, 63
tiredness 28
'to do' lists 69–71
'tool box' approach 10, 129–32
'turning the corner' 63

unanswered questions 92–8
  making sense of 'whys' 96, 97–9
  personal stories 93–4, 95, 97–8
unexpected death 14, 20, 45, 49, 72, 93–4, 200–1
  informing a child 150–1
unhelpful thoughts, challenging 75–83, 218, 231, 251–2
  anger 84–9
  framework 313–15
  guilt 80–2, 83
  regret 89–90
unhelpful/unrealistic advice and comments from others 33, 60, 61, 129, 162, 165–6, 169, 278–9, 281, 295–6
uniqueness of grief 5–6, 43, 276–7, 294

violent death 20, 73, 151, 191–2
voice messages 176–7
'volume control' for grief 37

wave-like pattern of grief 15, 21–5, 23–4, 31, 36, 63, 183, 257, 283–4, 285
  trigger waves 22, 180, 208, 218, 225, 257, 283, 284, 288
wedding and relationship anniversaries 232–4
wedding rings 180–1
weekends, coping with 119
withdrawal x, 133
work
  interacting with colleagues 170–1
  personal stories 117–19, 163, 171
  returning to 68, 117–19, 163
  telling colleagues about a bereavement 163
worry boxes 111
'wound analogy' 43, 133, 246, 285–6
writing to your loved one 53, 56–9